Goalkeeping Drills

volume two

Drills for improving technique, tactics and decision making.

by
Gerd Thissen
Klaus Röllgen

Library of Congress Cataloging - in - Publication Data

by Röllgen, Klaus and Thissen, Gerd
   Goalkeeping Drills: volume two
      Drills for improving technique, tactics and decision making.
ISBN No. 1-89094641-9
Library of Congress Catalog Number 00-101831
Copyright © April 2000

Originally printed in Germany - 1999 by Carolus-Sportverlag

Art Direction/Book Layout
Kimberly N. Bender

Diagrams
Karlheinz Grindler

Photos
Presse-Foto-Dienst

Original Layout in Germany
Carlus-Sportverlag

Editing and Proofing
Bryan R. Beaver

Printed by
DATA REPRODUCTIONS

REEDSWAIN INC
612 Pughtown Road • Spring City • Pennsylvania 19475
1-800-331-5191• www.reedswain.com

Goalkeeping Drills

volume two

Drills for improving technique, tactics and decision making.

by
Gerd Thissen
Klaus Röllgen

published by
REEDSWAIN INC

Foreword

I have often wished that I had a book of coaching drills for goalkeepers. When I watch training sessions, I am always surprised to see how little specific work is carried out with goalkeepers. Often the only time that a goalkeeper is called on to show what he can do is when a drill finishes up with a shot at goal. This cannot be described as systematic goalkeeper coaching.

Even coaches who devote time to their goalkeepers are amazingly lacking in ideas. Perhaps the soccer theorists have left coaches in the dark.

I am therefore grateful to Gerd Thissen and Klaus Röllgen for this contribution to meeting a clear need. This easily accessible book will stimulate many a voluntary helper to accept the role of goalkeeper coach. This aspect of the book is of particular significance for those at the lower or junior levels of the game, who may have to supervise the training of 15 players alone.

I hope that this book will become widely accepted by coaches at all levels and will lead to an improvement in the quality of goalkeeper coaching.

Egidius Braun
President of the German Soccer Association

We do not want to exaggerate. The soccer world is all too familiar with extravagant claims. However, it can be said with every justification that a goalkeeper occupies an important and special position in a soccer team. This should be reflected in goalkeeper coaching. It should be varied, focused and tough.

This book contains all the elements of good goalkeeper conditioning. I congratulate the authors and hope that coaches and goalkeepers will take its lessons to heart in daily practice.

Dettmar Cramer
German professional league, German Soccer Association and FIFA coach.

General and goalkeeper-specific general exercises - a basic and essential part of modern goalkeeper conditioning. A goalkeeper's defensive actions require a high level of flexibility, agility, dexterity and coordination, as for example when he is at full stretch to block a low shot with his foot.

Table of Contents

Introduction

Soccer goalkeeping requires good technique, a good tactical understanding and good physical fitness. Conditioning must repeatedly focus on all of these aspects, both individually and in combination, to enable goalkeepers to develop to their full potential. Unfortunately this is not always the case. Many coaches and instructors tend to concentrate on just a few elements of goalkeeping, which almost invariably concern only goal-line skills. Important aspects such as dominating the penalty area are rarely dealt with.

This book describes a number of widely varied drills, which are intended to improve the individual **key aspects of goalkeeping**. It contains a large selection of drills as well as describing various aids (tires, for example) with which imaginative goalkeeper training sessions can be devised.

The following drills are not meant to form an integrated coaching program. The intention is to give coaches a wide and varied selection of drills, so that they can plan their own programs to achieve their own objectives. The drills have been devised primarily with amateur soccer players in mind. Most of them involve only one goalkeeper, although a few are for two goalkeepers. A number of drills simulate match conditions and require the participation of outfield players. Drills that simply require the participation of a goalkeeper as an aid to improving the shooting skills of outfield players are not included.

It is assumed that the goalkeepers who perform the drills have already acquired the various elements of goalkeeping technique and have mastered the main principles of goalkeeping tactics. In principle the drills are within the capabilities of the average amateur goalkeeper.

The layout of the book derives from the wish to give the reader a visual impression of the described drill, thus making it easier to understand. Each description is accompanied by a number of diagrams, showing the key phases of the drill. This should enable coaches and instructors to translate them more easily into everyday coaching practice.

Key aspects of the drills

The **key aspects** of the following drills are derived from the **conditional, technical** and **tactical factors** that characterize **modern goalkeeping**. Even when outfield players are involved, only the goalkeeping aspects of the drill are described. Some of the drills are organized and simplified in such a way as to make them easier to understand.

The following **key aspects** are referred to in the practical part of the book.

Technique	Tactics	Conditioning
• Handling the ball	• Positional play	• Speed off the mark
• Catching technique	• Dominating the penalty area	• Reaction speed
• Gathering low balls	• Winning the ball	• Endurance
• Diving forward to catch the ball	• Moving off the line at the right moment	• Take-off strength
• Rolling sideways	• One against one situations	• Agility
• Diving to stop low shots	• Using technical and tactical skills in simulated match situations	• Coordination
• Diving to stop medium-high shots		
• Diving to stop high to medium-high shots		
• Punching (one hand and two hands)		
• Deflecting the ball		
• Throwing and kicking the ball into play		
• Kicking with the instep		
• Sidefooting the ball		
• Defending with the feet		

The general warming-up drills can only fulfill their purpose if they are carried out for the correct length of time. Otherwise the emphasis is on the following key aspects.

Endurance is only mentioned and singled out as a special conditioning objective in connection with a few drills, as endurance can be made the main aspect of almost any drill by increasing its duration.

When the focus is on take-off strength, the words "running take-off from one foot" will be added in parentheses when this is the main aspect of the drill.

The muscular conditioning aspects mentioned in connection with many drills are of secondary importance and are usually attributable to changes of position and posture during the course of the drill. The exclusive gymnastic objective is strengthening the muscles.

Goalkeeping Conditioning

Special conditioning

A key characteristic of goalkeeper conditioning is that it is mainly carried out **individually**. It can thus be regarded as special conditioning. In contrast to outfield players, goalkeepers carry out drills almost exclusively concerned with acquiring and developing the special skills and abilities they need to play in their position in the team. Like every other member of the team, the goalkeeper must acheive a certain basic level in the areas of **conditioning, technique** and **tactics** to be successful. Moreover he must have **special qualities** to be able to perform the tasks and meet the demands associated with his position. It is therefore necessary for a goalkeeper to be coached **separately** and **individually**. Comprehensive, varied and targeted coaching must be used to build up and develop the goalkeeper's innate movement skills. Only then can a goalkeeper acquire the **understanding of his role** that will enable him to carry out the basic tasks associated with his position within the framework of the team as a whole and the system it plays. Through appropriate **conditioning experience** he learns the basic principles associated with his position and is able to appreciate his conditional, technical and tactical resources correctly, so that he can apply them in simulated match situations and in real matches.

Organizational framework

For most coaches, goalkeeper coaching poses **problems of both content and organization**. During a training session a coach must keep both outfield players and goalkeepers busy with a variety of tasks. Because he cannot supervise both groups at the same time, he must ensure that there is no slacking on the part of the group with which he is not directly involved at any given time. Usually the goalkeepers find themselves left to their own devices for part of the time or simply have to stand around with nothing to do. The time that can be devoted to issues that are of direct relevance to goalkeepers, or to eliminating individual weaknesses, is short. Good organization is the best way to remedy this shortcoming. The following **organizational options** are available for goalkeeper training sessions.

- The coach spends time with the goalkeepers before or after the main training session.

In this case the coach might devote 45 minutes to working with his goal-keepers without having to observe his outfield players at the same time. The weather plays a role here. To avoid any risk of the goalkeepers catching a cold, they should be closely involved in the main training session when the weather is poor (when it is raining, during the winter, etc.). Periods of rest when wearing clothing that is soaked with rain or sweat should be avoided. If a session for goalkeepers is held after the main training session, the goalkeepers can be allowed to turn up in time for the second part of the main session. They can then warm up on their own before joining in with the other players.

- Goalkeeper conditioning is integrated into the main training session

The goalkeepers participate in the warming-up and the general conditioning work of the outfield players. Goalkeeper-specific aspects are introduced during shooting practice, when the goalkeepers are confronted with situations similar to those in a real match.

- The goalkeepers work on their own in line with a conditioning plan drawn up by the coach while the coach works with the other players.

This independent manner of working requires self-discipline and responsibility from the goalkeepers. The plan must be carefully prepared by the coach. The coach must discuss the drills with the goalkeepers to ensure that they are thoroughly familiar with them. To prevent any misunderstandings, the goalkeepers should have already carried out the drills under the supervision of the coach. To achieve his conditioning objectives the coach must specify the duration of the periods of work and rest.
It is worth remarking that excessive rivalry or feelings of antagonism between the first and second goalkeepers can impede this independent approach or even make it impossible. In this case it is advisable to give each goalkeeper his own conditioning plan and allow him to work independently.

- The coach supervises a complete training session with the goalkeepers.

The training session can be held on the same day as the outfield players' session (for example 2 hours beforehand), or on another day.

- While the chief coach supervises the main training session, the assistant coach supervises the goalkeepers.

If the training ground is big enough, this is the best way of ensuring intensive and effective goalkeeper conditioning. Moreover the goalkeepers can immediately be called upon to participate in the main training session when necessary.

There is no general answer to the question of which of these options is the best. In practice all of these options can be used. Naturally, circumstances at professional clubs differ from those in the amateur game. Amateur coaches are dependent on the free time that they and their goalkeepers can make available for additional training sessions. Ideally a goalkeeper requires the intensive supervision and help of a coach or assistant coach. Obviously this is not always feasible. It is, however, of considerable importance that a coach makes the best use of the available time and resources to plan a conditioning regime that will motivate his goalkeepers as much as possible. **Skillful alternation between the above forms of organization** can contribute to this.

General principles

- The intensity of the drills, the length of the recuperation periods, the number of repeats, etc. should always be harmonized to the level of conditioning of the goalkeeper and the coaching objectives.

In principle, the objectives of many drills can only be achieved if the drills are carried out intensively. Many of the drill descriptions indicate the suggested number of repeats in the form of the **number of balls** (for example, **6 balls = 6 repeats**). For drills carried out by pairs of players, the suggested **number of repeats** may be indicated directly (for example, **swap tasks after 5 repeats**).

- Adjust the degree of difficulty of the drill to the goalkeeper's level of conditioning and ability.

- Gradually increase the degree of difficulty and complexity of the drills, while gradually introducing drills that make higher technical and tactical demands on the goalkeeper.

- Training for technique and reaction speed should only be carried out when the goalkeepers are warmed up and rested.

Coordination conditioning

Goalkeeper-specific coordination conditioning involves **drills with the ball** that focus on a specific aspect of technique, supplemented by **additional tasks**. These additional tasks precede a defensive action by the goalkeeper. These may include various **forms of running** (forward, backward, sideways, hopping, etc.), different paths (straight line, zigzag, slalom, curve, etc.) and a variety of **positional and postural changes** (turning, rolling, jumping, goalkeeper lying face down, on his back, front, side, etc.) either individually or in combination. Variety is of the essence, so that the goalkeeper is faced with constantly changing challenges to his sense of orientation or balance, his reaction speed, etc. This book contains numerous examples and variations.

Competitive drills

Competitive drills can be used to make goalkeeper conditioning more varied and interesting. In addition, the **competitive element** of the drill stimulates the goalkeeper's motivation and readiness to learn and perform well. A genuinely competitive situation is created, which promotes the goalkeeper's will to win and creates opportunities to use the techniques and tactics he has learned and practiced. The main objective of these competitive drills is to give the goalkeeper the opportunity to employ his abilities to the limit, especially in one-against-one situations. This means that the goalkeeper must always have a reasonable chance of saving the ball when the coach or outfield player tries to score. Despite the competitive element, the emphasis is on the **goalkeeper's performance** and not the shooting ability of the outfield player or the coach.

General exercises for goalkeepers

Keeping goal makes considerable demands on a goalkeeper's athletic prowess. Strength, speed and endurance have to be allied with robustness, agility, dexterity and excellent coordination to enable a goalkeeper to respond adequately to the challenges of all types of match situations by diving, rolling, jumping, getting back quickly onto his feet and reacting instantaneously without risking injury, irrespective of the weather and pitch conditions. **General and goalkeeper-specific exercises** are therefore a basic and indispensable part of modern goalkeeper conditioning. Gymnastic exercises for the arm, leg and trunk muscles and the associated ligaments, tendons and joints, as well as whole-body exercises, build up the goalkeeper's body in general and can be targeted on facilitating the many movements that a goalkeeper may need to make. One example is the leg stretch to block a low ball. Gymnastic exercises suitable for working out alone or in pairs, with or without aids, can be incorporated into the warming-up phase or recuperation periods as a supplementary active element of goalkeeper training sessions. A few gymnastic exercises are described in this book. They are carried out with the help of a ball and should make the training sessions more positive and enjoyable for the players. The conditioning effect is usually based on short, intensive periods of work involving a lot of movement. This effect can be enhanced by using a medicine ball instead of an ordinary soccer ball.

Outfield play

Since the recent introduction of the backpass rule, greater demands have been made on the ability of the goalkeeper to function as an outfield player. As well as practicing their own specific skills, goalkeepers should train together with the other players as often as possible to learn **ball technique** and the **tactical aspects of outfield play**. When a goalkeeper plays in an outfield position during a training session he learns about aspects of play such as the different lines of the ball and the outfield players' runs and patterns of movement. This can help him to anticipate an attacker's intentions. The experience that a goalkeeper gains in this way gives him a better understanding of the demands of specific outfield positions and helps him to improve his cooperation with his teammates and adjust more readily to the opposing team's attacking tactics.

Indoor training sessions

During autumn and winter the weather and the condition of the pitch may considerably restrict the opportunities for goalkeepers to train outdoors. If the pitch is frozen, for example, there is a much higher risk of sustaining an injury when diving to stop the ball. Indoor training for goalkeepers is often regarded unfavorably and is viewed as a last resort. Nevertheless, a gymnasium presents opportunities that are either not present outdoors or could only be made available with considerable effort. With appropriate **organizational preparation**, indoor sessions can supplement and enhance outdoor training sessions. The focus should be on the following **key conditioning aspects**.

Gymnastic exercises

A varied and comprehensive range of gymnastic drills and exercises, both with and without apparatus, is available for goalkeepers. Gymnastic balls, medicine balls, bars and clubs can be used as well as mats, wall bars, etc. Working with gymnastic apparatus increases the goalkeeper's motivation as well as the effect of the individual exercises. The overall result is that all aspects of the goalkeeper's physique are improved. He can carry out exercises while lying face down or on his back without any fear of catching a cold. A richly varied conditioning program can be put together by combining different elements in different ways, with the focus on developing his agility, dexterity and mobility.

General and specific physical conditioning

A gymnasium offers almost unlimited opportunities for improving a goalkeeper's physical condition. All kinds of walking, running, hopping, climbing and crawling exercises can be carried out. Running and jumping, working with a medicine ball, different types of circuit training, etc. permit varied and targeted physical conditioning.

Technique

Despite the hard floor, almost all goal-stopping techniques can be practiced in the gymnasium in a variety of ways. The use of mats on the floor, in combination with padding in the goalkeeper's shorts and sweater, make falling and diving possible to almost the same extent as on a grass pitch. A ball can also be suspended from the supports used for gymnastic rings to allow the goalkeepers to practice one and two-fisted punching.

Speed of reaction and movement

Large areas of the walls of the gymnasium can often be used for shooting practice. They offer many possibilities for goalkeepers to sharpen their reaction speed and to practice alone. They can also be used to develop and improve catching skills.

Coordination

The markings and apparatus in the gymnasium offer numerous organizational possibilities for practicing coordination skills. For example, a goalkeeper can be required to complete a small obstacle course before preventing another player from scoring.

Simple and available aids and apparatus

The use of different aids and apparatus for goalkeeper training sessions simplifies the coach's task of making the sessions varied and interesting. The structure of the sessions can be modified in many ways and can be targeted on developing particular skills and abilities. The aids and apparatus also give goalkeepers **more options for working on their own**, especially for **practicing technique**. In general, the use of complex structural aids should be avoided. Everything that can be found in **any sports facility** should be used, e.g. a suspended ball, a sandpit, the pitch, the steps of the bleachers, a "shooting wall." Other aids that can be easily obtained include weighted vests, dumbbells, expanders, hurdles, swingballs, rugby balls or used tires.

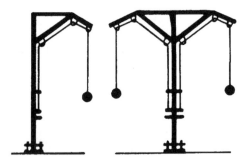

A suspended ball is an excellent aid for goalkeepers practicing alone. It is especially suitable for learning how to punch the ball with one or both fists. Because this can be practiced repeatedly, it is an especially effective method of learning and improving this skill. A suspended ball can also be used to condition a goalkeeper's take-off strength. The cord to which the ball is attached should be as long as possible to ensure that the goalkeeper acquires a good punching technique. The long swing of the ball allows the goalkeeper to concentrate on his punching technique and to become used to assessing the path of the ball.

The pitch, the bleachers, weighted vests and hurdles can be used in a variety of ways during goalkeeper training sessions. **Diving** should first be practiced in a sandpit to break down any inhibitions the goalkeeper may have and avoid accidents. A sandpit also provides an excellent soft surface for **conditioning and take-off exercises**. For this reason, many of the drills that are carried out on grass should also be carried out in a sandpit.

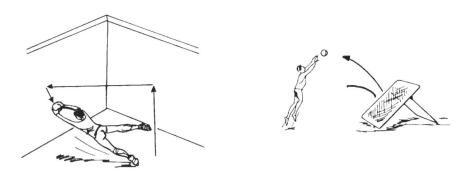

Part of the wall of the changing room or the wall around the sports ground can be used as a shooting wall. If there is no grass in front of the wall, sand can be spread to reduce the risk of injury. If a portable shooting wall made of wood or some other equipment is used, it should not cushion the ball on impact and thus rob it of some of its momentum. A goalkeeper can **practice alone** in a variety of ways with such a wall. In particular he can develop and improve his **reaction speed** and **catching technique**. A shooting wall with an uneven surface increases the degree of difficulty for the goalkeeper. The direction of the rebound cannot be predicted and the goalkeeper has to react with the speed of lightning.

A new variation of the shooting wall is the **kickback**. The angle of the rebound surface can be varied, so the angle of rebound also varies. This provides the coach with numerous options to suit the level of ability of the goalkeeper.

An oval **rugby ball** can be used to improve the goalkeeper's **catching technique** and **reaction speed**. The ball is also relatively heavy, so the goalkeeper has to grasp it firmly when he catches it. The shape of the ball makes its flight more irregular and difficult to gauge than that of a round ball.

Used **tires** are very worthwhile aids for goalkeeper training sessions. They can be stacked to form an obstacle that the goalkeeper has to dive over, and they are used above all to improve the goalkeeper's **endurance, take-off strength, agility** and **dexterity**. Since there is little danger of suffering an injury when diving over tires, goalkeepers easily overcome any psychological inhibitions they may have about diving over other forms of obstacle (e.g. hurdles).

The descriptions of the **basic drills** are organized in accordance with a **basic structure**. The descriptions are subdivided into the following elements: **Key aspects, Starting Position, Phase 1, Phase 2**, etc., **Number of participants** and **Equipment**. In some cases **variations** of the basic drill are included. Each variation is described individually. The starting position, phase 1, phase 2, etc. and variations are illustrated by the use of **diagrams**.

Example

Key aspects
- Catching technique
- Agility
- Diving to stop low shots
- Diving to stop high to medium-high shots
- Rolling away to the side

- Take-off strength
- Reaction speed
- Catching the ball securely

Variation 2
- Two-fisted punching

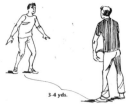

3-4 yds.

Starting position
The goalkeeper stands 3 or 4 yards from the coach, who is holding the ball.

Phase 1
The coach drops the ball and kicks it hard to the goalkeeper, varying the height and direction of the ball.

Phase 2
The goalkeeper must catch or stop the shots, which can come at him at all heights and be directed at his body or to his right or left. He must use the correct catching technique and secure the ball properly after catching it. He throws the ball back into the coach's hands and then resumes his starting position, so that the coach can immediately kick the ball to him again.

Variations
1. The goalkeeper kneels instead of standing, so the coach has to take care not to kick the ball too high or too wide of him.
2. The coach kicks the ball straight at the goalkeeper and the goalkeeper punches it away with both fists.

• Catching technique

Participants:	1 goalkeeper	Equipment:	1 ball
	Coach	Variation 2:	5 balls

The text in the **margin** is intended as an aid to the reader when he is searching for the correct type of drill.

Example: • Catching technique

This text indicates how the drills are organized. It shows the **specific objective of the described drill**. This may be:

- Handling the ball
- Catching technique
- Agility
- Endurance
- Take-off strength
- Reaction speed
- Defending with the feet
- Punching the ball

- Deflecting the ball
- Winning the ball
- Throwing and kicking the ball into play
- Positional play
- One against one situations
- Dominating the penalty area

Each of these objectives can in turn be assigned to one of the following categories:

- General exercises with the ball
- Competitive situations and simulated match situations
- Competitive games
- Conditioning aids

Detailed information on the technical, tactical and conditioning objectives of the drill is given under the heading **Key aspects**. These key aspects refer to the basic drill.

Example

Key aspects
- Catching technique
- Agility
- Diving to stop low shots
- Diving to stop high to medium-high shots

- Rolling away to the side
- Take-off strength
- Reaction speed
- Catching the ball securely

The sequence of key aspects indicates to some extent the weighting of the objectives. The most important aspect is positioned first. If the basic drill is supplemented by one or more variations, their key aspects are also listed. The key aspects already listed for the basic drill are not repeated, as they usually also to apply for the variations.

Example

Key aspects
- Catching technique
- Agility
- Diving to stop low shots
- Diving to stop high to medium-high shots
- Rolling away to the side
- Take-off strength
- Reaction speed
- Catching the ball securely

Variation
- Two-fisted punching

The information needed to understand the selected drill is given under the headings **Starting position**, **Phase 1**, **Phase 2**, etc. and, for the variations, under **Variation** or **Variations**. The texts under these headings, together with the **illustrations**, form a complete unit. The text of each drill is formulated as an accompaniment to the diagrams and can be used as an aid to a **verbal explanation** of the drill. This is important for coaches and instructors, who must not only be able to understand a drill before putting it into practice but must also be able to explain it precisely to their players and point out any difficulties they may encounter. The ability to describe a drill to the goalkeeper and to translate the description into practice is essential if the objective of the drill is to be achieved. This is why the illustrations are accompanied by detailed and comprehensive descriptions. Each drill should be regarded as complete in itself. The text contains no references to other drills. This makes a certain amount of repetition unavoidable. Each description refers to possible difficulties that may be encountered and to opportunities for emphasizing specific aspects. As already mentioned, these are important for the proper implementation of the drill and for the targeted realization and intensification of the effects of the drill. The **variations** usually involve a higher level of complexity or difficulty. They demand more from the goalkeeper. If more than one variation is given, they are listed in order of increasing difficulty.

The descriptions also include information on the number of **participants** and the **equipment** needed, including goal area, half of the pitch, goal, barrier, etc.

Example

Participants:	1 goalkeeper	Equipment:	1 ball
	Coach	Variation 2:	5 balls

The **basic structure** of a drill can be varied as required. Markings can be changed or added. Flags, cones or balls can be used as goalposts. The locations where the drills are carried out can be varied. The specified number of balls, size of goal, distance between coach and goalkeeper and between goalkeeper and ball should always be understood as guidelines. Coaches are free to make changes in line with their own ideas. In many cases a second goalkeeper can take over the role of the coach, and in his turn the coach can assume the role of the second goalkeeper if necessary. The basic structure can thus be followed closely or broadened at will to include or focus on individual objectives related to the goalkeeper's strengths and weaknesses. With a little initiative and imagination the basic drills can be used as a model for new drills or variations. Many variations have not been included in the book, since its purpose is to introduce as many different types of drills as possible rather than elaborate at length on just a few.

Key to diagrams

Path of the ball

Path of the player running with the ball

Path of player running off the ball

o   Ball

Marker flag

Line marking part of the pitch (goal line, side line, center line, lines marking the goal area or penalty area)

Direction of turn

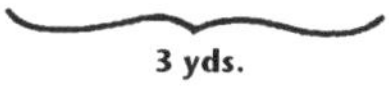

Distance

3 yds.

Defender

Outfield player, attacker

Neutral midfield player

• Defending with the feet

Key aspects
- Defending with the feet
- Agility
- Take-off strength
- Reaction speed

Starting position
The goalkeeper stands in the middle of the goal, facing the coach, who is standing 6 yards in front of the goal and is holding a ball in each hand.

Phase 1
The coach throws both balls simultaneously at the same height to the goalkeeper. With his right hand he throws the ball to the goalkeeper's left, and with his left hand to the goalkeeper's right. The goalkeeper must be able to reach both balls.

Phase 2
The goalkeeper dives to one side and tries to stop one ball with his hand and the other with his foot. The coach gathers the ball and the goalkeeper resumes his starting position, and so on.

Variation
1. The coach calls out to the goalkeeper, specifying which ball he has to stop with his foot.
2. The coach throws one ball at knee height and the other at shoulder height. The goalkeeper must use his foot to return the lower ball to the coach.
3. The goalkeeper stands with his back to the coach. The coach calls out and then throws the balls. The goalkeeper must turn quickly and stop the balls.

Participants:	1 goalkeeper	Equipment:	2 balls
	Coach		1 goal

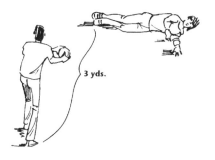

Starting position
The goalkeeper lies on his side with his arms stretched out in front of his shoulders so that he cannot use his arms to press himself off the ground. The coach stands 3 yards away, level with the goalkeeper's feet.

Phase 1
The coach rolls the ball or throws it at a height of up to 18 inches toward the goalkeeper's feet.

Phase 2
The goalkeeper tries to kick the ball toward the coach. The coach gathers the ball and rolls or throws it back to the goalkeeper, and so on.

• Defending with the feet

Participants:	1 goalkeeper	Equipment: 1 ball
	Coach	

18

Key aspects
- Defending with the feet
- Agility
- Take-off strength
- Reaction speed

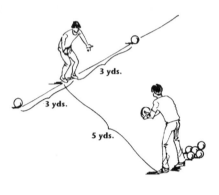

3 yds.

3 yds.

5 yds.

Starting position
The goalkeeper stands facing the coach, who is standing 5 yards away. 3 yards to either side of the goalkeeper is a ball. The coach holds a ball and there are 5 balls on the ground beside him.

Phase 1
The coach calls out "right" or "left" and the goalkeeper dives to the ball at that side. At the same time the coach throws a ball close to the other side, close enough for the goalkeeper to stop it with his feet. The coach varies the direction, height and speed of the throw.

links

Phase 2
As the goalkeeper dives, he tries to kick the ball thrown by the coach as far away as possible. The goalkeeper resumes his starting position and the coach picks up another ball, and so on.

Variation
The coach stands 10 yards away from the goalkeeper and shoots instead of throwing the ball.

Defending with the feet

Participants: 1 goalkeeper	Equipment: 8 balls
Coach	

Starting position
Goalkeepers A and B stand facing each other 10 yards apart. Goalkeeper A holds a ball.

Phase 1
Goalkeeper A throws the ball high to medium-high to goalkeeper B.
Goalkeeper B dives and punches the ball away to the side.

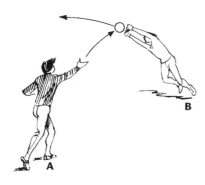

Phase 2
Goalkeeper B immediately leaps to his feet, sprints after the ball and gathers it. He throws it to goalkeeper A, who dives and punches it away to the side, and so on.

Variation
Goalkeeper A sprints after the ball that goalkeeper B has punched away and tries to catch it before it touches the ground or at least after the first bounce. Goalkeeper A then returns the ball to goalkeeper B, and so on.
After 10 throws the goalkeepers swap roles.

• Punching the ball

Key aspects
- Two-fisted punching
- Take-off strength
  (running one-footed take-off)
- Throwing the ball into play
- Speed off the mark

Starting position
Goalkeeper A stands facing the coach from a distance of 15 yards. The coach holds a ball. Goalkeeper B stands to the side of the coach.

Phase 1
The coach lets the ball fall and volleys it high to goalkeeper A, who runs and jumps to catch it. At the same time goalkeeper B starts a run to the right or left of goalkeeper A. He must change his position each time the coach plays the ball to goalkeeper A.

Phase 2
Goalkeeper A punches the ball into the path of goalkeeper B. Goalkeeper B controls the ball while the coach takes a few steps back until he is 15 yards from goalkeeper A again.

Phase 3
Goalkeeper B picks up the ball and throws it overarm to the coach. The coach catches it and plays it immediately to goalkeeper A, who is on his feet again, and so on. After 10 cycles the goalkeepers swap roles

• Punching the ball

Participants: 2 goalkeepers Coach	Equipment: 1 ball

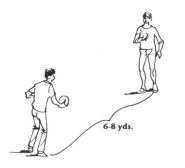

Starting position

The goalkeeper and the coach stand facing each other 6 to 8 yards apart.

Phase 1

The coach throws the ball medium-high to the goalkeeper. The goalkeeper dives forward and punches the ball back to the coach.

Phase 2

The coach takes a few steps back until he is again 6 to 8 yards away. While the goalkeeper is still on the ground the coach throws the ball medium-high to him again, and so on.

Variation

A second goalkeeper joins in, who stands in the coach's position. The coach stands 5 yards to the right and throws the ball. The second goalkeeper, for whom this is an active recuperation break, has the task of stopping the ball when the first goalkeeper punches it away and returning it to the coach. The first goalkeeper should punch the ball 2 or 3 yards to the side of the second goalkeeper so that he can dive to catch it.

• Punching the ball

Participants:	1 goalkeeper	Equipment:	1 ball
	Coach		
Variation:	2 goalkeepers		

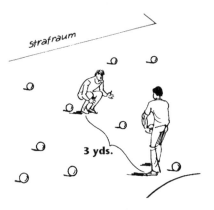

Starting position
The goalkeeper squats facing the coach from a distance of 3 yards. The coach holds the ball. The two are between the edge of the penalty area and the center line. The other balls lie distributed on the ground in this area, 5 to 10 yards apart.

Phase 1
The coach throws the ball high to medium-high to the right or left of the goalkeeper. The goalkeeper dives and punches the ball away to the side.

Phase 2
The coach runs to the nearest ball, picks it up and throws it to the goalkeeper as soon as he is on his feet again, and so on.

Variation
A goalkeeper punches the ball away to the side with one fist.

Punching the ball

Participants:	1 goalkeeper	Equipment:	10 balls
	Coach		1 half of the field

Key aspects
- One-fisted punching
- Diving to stop high to medium-high balls
- Take-off strength
- Catching the ball securely
- Throwing the ball into play

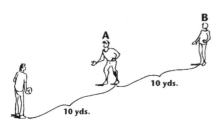

Starting position

The coach and goalkeeper B stand facing each other 20 yards apart. Goalkeeper A stands halfway between them facing the coach, who holds the ball.

Phase 1

The coach throws the ball in a high arc over goalkeeper A, so that it falls behind goalkeeper A.

Phase 2

Goalkeeper A turns, jumps and punches the ball with one fist toward goalkeeper B, who tries to catch it high in the air or before it bounces more than once.

• Punching the ball

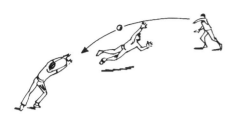

Phase 3

Goalkeeper B throws the ball overarm over goalkeeper A's head to the coach. Goalkeeper A tries to reach the ball. As soon as goalkeeper A has resumed his starting position the coach throws the ball again, and so on.

After 10 cycles the goalkeepers swap roles.

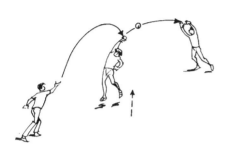

Variations

1. The coach and goalkeeper B swap positions.

2. Goalkeeper A does not turn to punch the ball but remains facing the coach and stretches backward as he jumps.

Punching the ball

Participants: 2 goalkeepers
Coach

Equipment: 1 ball

Key aspects
- Two-fisted punching
- Take-off strength
- Speed off the mark

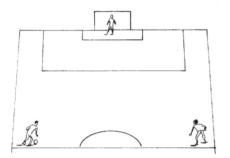

Starting position

The goalkeeper stands in the goal. The outfield player and the coach stand about 20 yards outside the penalty area near the right and left sidelines. The coach has a ball at his feet.

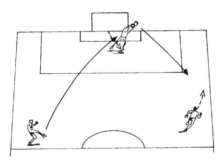

Phase 1

The coach kicks a high diagonal shot toward the far post. The goalkeeper moves off his line, jumps and punches the ball two-fisted into the path of the outfield player, who is making a forward run down the wing.

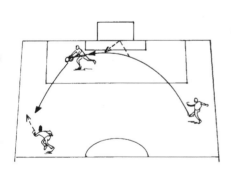

Phase 2

The outfield player controls the ball. As soon as the goalkeeper is in the goal again, the outfield player hits a high cross to the far post. The goalkeeper punches this into the path of the coach, who is making a forward run down the wing, and so on.

Punching the ball

Variation

The coach and the outfield player each have a ball. They alternately play high balls toward the near post. The goalkeeper punches each ball back into the path of the kicker. The coach and the outfield player make their runs down the wing or into the center of the pitch.

Participants:	1 goalkeeper	**Equipment:**	1 ball
	1 outfield player		1 goal
	Coach		1 half of the field
		Variation:	2 balls

Key aspects	
• Two-fisted punching	• Take-off strength (running one-footed take-off)
• Agility	• Reaction speed
• Diving to stop low balls	• Catching the ball securely
• Diving to stop high to medium-high balls	• Deflecting the ball
• Rolling away to the side	• Throwing the ball into play
	• Speed off the mark

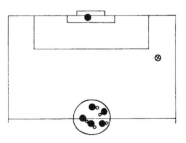

Starting position

The goalkeeper stands in the goal. The outfield players each have a ball, which they dribble about in the center circle. The coach stands at the right corner of the penalty area. He observes, directs and corrects the players.

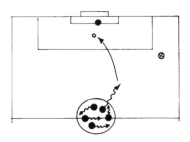

Phase 1

At a call from the coach, one of the outfield players dribbles forward out of the center circle and strikes a high ball that should fall between the penalty spot and the goal.

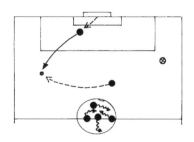

Phase 2

The goalkeeper comes off his line and jumps to meet the ball, which he punches two-fisted into the path of the outfield player, who is making a forward run to right or left or down the middle of the pitch.

Punching the ball

29

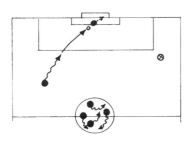

Phase 3

As the goalkeeper returns to his goal, the outfield player controls the ball, pushes it forward and immediately shoots at the goal. He must not touch the ball more than 3 times in this sequence. The goalkeeper stops the shot. He must catch it securely in both hands.

Phase 4

The goalkeeper throws the ball into the path of the outfield player, who runs toward the other side of the pitch after shooting. The outfield player controls the ball and runs back to the center line with it. Meanwhile the coach has called out to the next player to start his run.

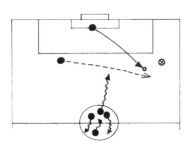

Phase 4 is not carried out if the goalkeeper can only deflect the ball or fails to reach it at all. In this case the outfield player retrieves the ball and sprints with it along the sideline to the center line.

Key to symbols:

- ●   Goalkeeper, outfield player
- ⊗   Coach
- ○   Ball

Participants:	1 goalkeeper	**Equipment:**	5 balls
	5 outfield players		1 goal
	Coach		penalty area
			center circle

• Punching the ball

Key aspects
- One-fisted punching
- Two-fisted punching
- Winning the ball

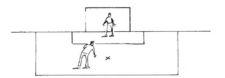

Starting position

The goalkeeper stands in the goal. The coach stands beside the penalty spot. The outfield player is on the right wing with a ball at his feet.

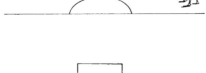

Phase 1

The outfield player crosses a high ball to the coach in front of the goal and runs immediately toward the center of the pitch.

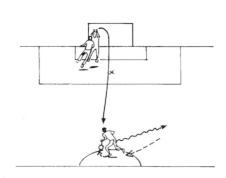

Phase 2

The goalkeeper comes off his line and punches the ball either one-fisted or two-fisted into the path of the outfield player. The coach jumps as if to head the cross, but plays a mainly passive role. The outfield player controls the ball, runs with it at his feet toward the right wing and crosses the ball high again, and so on.

• Punching the ball

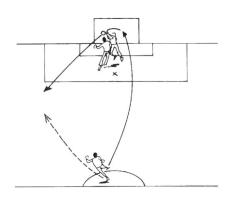

Variation
1. The coach challenges the goalkeeper for the cross and tries to head the ball into goal.

2. The outfield player starts in the vicinity of the center circle and hits the ball high down the middle of the pitch toward the goal, then runs toward the wing to receive the ball when the goalkeeper punches it.

● **Punching the ball**

Participants:	1 goalkeeper	**Equipment:**	1 ball
	1 outfield player		1 goal
	Coach		1 half of the field

Starting position

The goalkeeper stands in the goal, facing the coach, who is on the goal line 1 yard outside the goalkeeper's left-hand post. The coach is holding a ball and there are another 9 balls on the ground nearby.

Phase 1

The coach throws the ball up high so that it falls toward the cross bar. He throws the balls to the near post, the far post and the center of the goal in random sequence.

Phase 2

The goalkeeper moves to get under the falling ball and jumps to flick it powerfully over the bar with one hand. He returns quickly to the center of the goal and the coach throws the next ball, and so on.

• Deflecting the ball

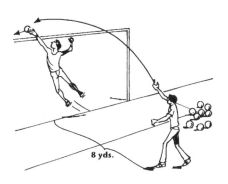

8 yds.

Variation
The coach stands 8 yards in front of the goal. He again throws the ball up high so that it falls toward the cross bar to the right or left of the goal-keeper or directly behind him.

• Deflecting the ball

Participants: 1 goalkeeper	**Equipment:**	10 balls
Coach		1 goal
		1 goal area

Starting position
The goalkeeper stands in the middle of the goal. The coach stands on the penalty spot, holding a ball. Another 5 balls lie on the ground nearby.

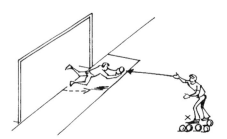

Phase 1
The coach throws the ball medium-high so that it would bounce in the goal area. The goalkeeper sprints forward and dives to catch the ball before it touches the ground.

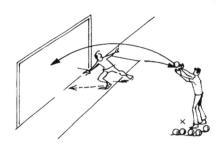

Phase 2
The goalkeeper throws the ball back to the coach and sprints back to the goal line. At the same time the coach throws the next ball in an arc so that falls toward the crossbar.

● Deflecting the ball

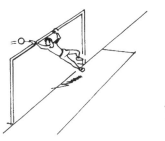

Phase 3

The goalkeeper jumps backward and flicks the ball over the bar with one hand. He then resumes his starting position and the coach picks up the next ball, and so on.

Variations

1. In both cases the coach throws the ball to the right or left of the goalkeeper.

2. The coach throws the first ball so that the goalkeeper has to run about 8 yards out of his goal to catch it. The goalkeeper throws the ball back to the coach and immediately performs a backward roll. The coach waits until the he completes this before throwing the next ball.

• Deflecting the ball

Participants:	1 goalkeeper	Equipment:	6 balls
	Coach		1 goal
			1 goal area

Key aspects
- Deflecting the ball
- Agility
- Diving to stop high to medium-high balls
- Diving forward and catching the ball

- Take-off strength
- Catching the ball securely
- Speed off the mark

Variations 1 and 2
- Reaction speed

Deflecting the ball

Starting position
The goalkeeper stands in the middle of the goal. The coach stands on the penalty spot, holding a ball. Another ball lies on the ground 8 yards from the goal, between the coach and the goalkeeper. Another 6 balls are on the ground near the coach.

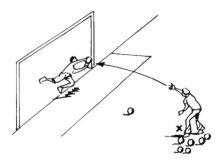

Phase 1
The coach throws the ball low to the goalkeeper's left. The goalkeeper dives, catches it in both hands and clutches it securely to his body.

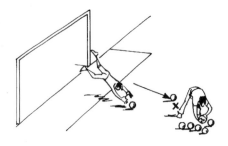

Phase 2
The goalkeeper rolls the ball back to the coach and dives forward to grasp the ball positioned in front of the goal, clutching it securely to his body. At the same time the coach picks up the next ball.

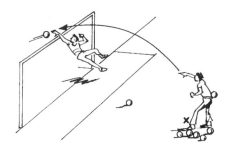

Phase 3

The goalkeeper replaces the ball in its original position and the coach throws the next ball in a high arc so that it falls toward the crossbar. The goalkeeper backpedals, jumps backward and flicks the ball over the bar with one hand. He then resumes his starting position and the coach picks up the next ball, and so on.

Variations

1. The goalkeeper punches the falling ball one-handed over the crossbar or wide of the goalpost.

2. The coach throws the first ball medium-high or bounces it at the goal.

3. The coach throws the first ball toward the corner of the goal, so that the goalkeeper can only deflect it wide of the post.

Deflecting the ball

Participants: 1 goalkeeper	Equipment: 8 balls
Coach	1 goal

Key aspects	• Reaction speed

Key aspects
- Deflecting the ball
- Agility
- Diving to stop high to medium-high balls
- Rolling away to the side
- Take-off strength

- Reaction speed
- Speed off the mark
- Positional play

Variation 2
- Punching the ball

Variation 6
- Catching the ball securely

Starting position

The goalkeeper squats in the goal close to his right-hand post. He is facing the coach, who stands at the corner of the goal area holding a ball. Another 5 balls are on the ground nearby.

Phase 1

The coach throws the ball low to the goalkeeper's right. The goalkeeper dives to the side and grasps the ball in both hands.

Phase 2

While still on the ground the goalkeeper throws the ball back to the coach. He resumes his starting position as the coach catches the ball.

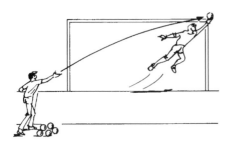

Phase 3

After the coach has thrown the ball one to three times to the goalkeeper's right, he calls out and throws the ball toward the goalkeeper's top left-hand corner. The goalkeeper dives and deflects the ball over the bar or wide of the goal.

• Deflecting the ball

Phase 4

The goalkeeper sprints back to his starting position. The coach picks up the next ball, and so on.

Variations

1. The coach does not call out before throwing the ball toward the top corner of the goal.

2. The goalkeeper punches the ball over the bar or wide of the goal.

3. The coach does not throw any low balls but throws the ball toward the top corner of the goal every time.

4. The coach throws the first ball toward the top corner. After the goalkeeper has deflected it wide of the goal the coach rolls the second ball toward the other corner. The goalkeeper runs back and dives to grasp it. He then throws it back to the coach, who immediately throws it toward the top corner again.

5. The coach rolls the first ball along the line marking the side of the goal area so that the goalkeeper has to leap and roll over to his right to grasp the ball. The coach throws the second ball low toward the goalkeeper's bottom right-hand corner and the third toward the top left-hand corner. The goalkeeper remains constantly in motion.

6. The coach throws the ball closer to the goalkeeper's left so that he can dive and catch it with both hands.

Deflecting the ball

Participants: 1 goalkeeper	**Equipment:** 6 balls
Coach	1 goal
	1 goal area

Key aspects	Variation 1
• Deflecting the ball	• Diving to stop high to
• Agility	medium-high balls
• Take-off strength	**Variation 2**
	• One-fisted punching

Starting position

The goalkeeper sits in the middle of the goal with his legs apart. The coach stands facing him 5 yards away. The coach is holding a ball and another 5 balls are on the ground nearby.

Phase 1

The coach throws the ball in a high arc so that it falls just below the bar, either above or slightly to one side of the goalkeeper.

Phase 2

The goalkeeper leaps to his feet and jumps up to deflect the ball over the bar. He then returns to his starting position, and so on.

Variations

1. The coach throws the ball high to medium-high about 2 yards to the side of the goalkeeper. The goalkeeper tries to deflect the ball wide of the post.
2. The goalkeeper punches the ball over the bar or wide of the goal with one fist.

Participants: 1 goalkeeper	**Equipment:** 6 balls
Coach	1 goal

Key aspects
- Winning the ball
- Take-off strength
- Catching the ball securely

Variantion 2
- One-fisted punching
- Two-fisted punching

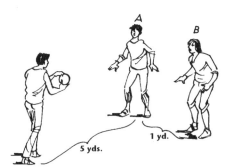

Starting position
Goalkeepers A and B stand 1 yard apart facing the coach, who stands 5 yards away holding a ball.

Phase 1
The coach throws the ball in an arc toward goalkeeper A. Both goalkeepers move toward the ball.

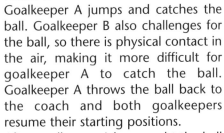

Phase 2
Goalkeeper A jumps and catches the ball. Goalkeeper B also challenges for the ball, so there is physical contact in the air, making it more difficult for goalkeeper A to catch the ball. Goalkeeper A throws the ball back to the coach and both goalkeepers resume their starting positions.
After goalkeeper A has caught the ball ten times the goalkeepers swap roles.

Variations
1. Goalkeeper B tries to head the ball away before goalkeeper A catches it.
2. An outfield player joins goalkeeper B in challenging for the ball. Depending on the situation, goalkeeper A catches the ball or punches it away with one or both fists.

• Winning the ball

Participants: 2 goalkeepers	Equipment: 1 ball
Coach	
Variation: 1 outfield player	

Key aspects
- Winning the ball
- Diving to stop low balls

- Diving to stop high to medium-high balls
- Take-off strength
- Reaction speed

Starting position
Goalkeeper A stands 1 yard behind goalkeeper B. The coach stands holding a ball 5 yards in front of goalkeeper B.

Phase 1
The coach throws the ball low, high or medium-high toward goalkeeper B, whose task is to impede goalkeeper A's view of the ball and block his direct route to it.

Phase 2
Goalkeeper A runs alternately right and left round goalkeeper B and dives to catch the ball, clutching it securely to his body. He then throws the ball back to the coach and resumes his starting position, and so on.

After goalkeeper A has caught the ball ten times the goalkeepers swap roles.

• Winning the ball

4.

Variations

1. Goalkeeper B also moves toward the ball and tries to block goalkeeper A's path while still giving him a chance to get to the ball.

2. The coach stands 10 yards away from goalkeeper B and volleys or half-volleys the ball at him. If the ball rebounds, both goalkeepers go after it.

3. Goalkeeper A stands 2 yards behind goalkeeper B. As soon as the coach serves the ball, goalkeeper B turns to face goalkeeper A and tries to block his path to the ball.

4. The coach throws the ball low to the side of the goalkeepers. Goalkeeper A dives to grasp the ball while goalkeeper B turns toward the ball and tries to control it with his foot. Goalkeeper A clutches the ball securely to his body with both hands.

• Winning the ball

Participants: 2 goalkeepers
Coach

Equipment: 1 ball

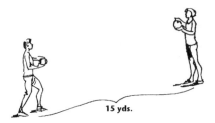

15 yds.

Starting position
The goalkeepers stand facing each other 15 yards apart. Each holds a ball.

Phase 1
They throw the balls to each other simultaneously at chest height.

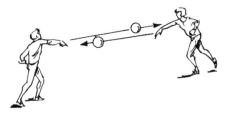

Phase 2
The goalkeepers catch the balls and roll them back to each other simultaneously.

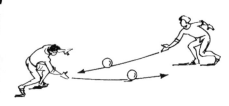

• Throwing and kicking the ball into play

Phase 3

The goalkeepers run after the rolling balls and dive and grasp them, clutching them securely to their chests. The goalkeepers then stand up again, each in the other's starting position, and so on.

Variations

1. The goalkeepers throw the balls slightly to the left or right of each other, so that they have to dive to stop them.

2. The goalkeepers bounce the balls at each other.

3. The goalkeepers stand 30 yards apart and throw the balls overarm to each other. Phases 2 and 3 remain the same.

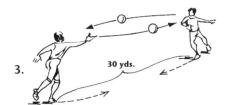

30 yds.

Participants: 2 goalkeepers   **Equipment:** 2 balls

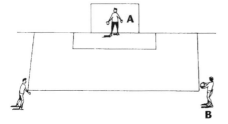

Starting position
Goalkeeper A stands in the goal. Goalkeeper B and the coach stand at the corners of the penalty area to his right and left respectively. Goalkeeper B is holding a ball.

Phase 1
Goalkeeper B throws the ball hard and low at the goal, trying to score. Goalkeeper A tries to stop the ball, catching it securely in both hands.

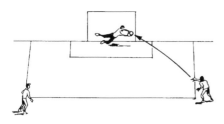

Phase 2
Goalkeeper A rolls the ball toward the coach and sprints after it.

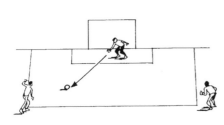

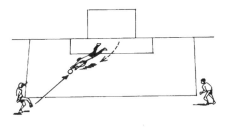

Phase 3

The coach plays the ball straight back to goalkeeper A, varying the height, strength and direction each time. The aim is for goalkeeper A to be forced to dive for the ball from a running start. In any case goalkeeper A must be outside the goal area when he tries to grasp the ball.

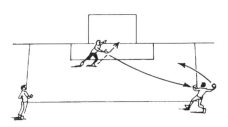

Phase 4

Goalkeeper A throws the ball from hip height to goalkeeper B and sprints back to the goal. Goalkeeper B catches the ball and immediately throws it at goal again, and so on.

After 5 cycles the goalkeepers swap roles.

● **Throwing and kicking the ball into play**

Participants: 2 goalkeepers	**Equipment:** 1 ball
Coach	1 goal
	penalty area

Key aspects
- Kicking the ball into play
- Throwing the ball into play
- Take-off strength
- Catching the ball securely
- Speed off the mark

• Throwing and kicking the ball into play

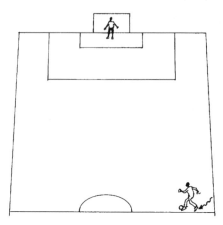

Starting position
The goalkeeper stands in the goal. The coach runs with a ball at his feet in the vicinity of the center line.

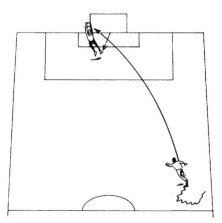

Phase 1
The coach crosses the ball high in front of the goal. The goalkeeper comes out to meet the ball, jumps and catches it.

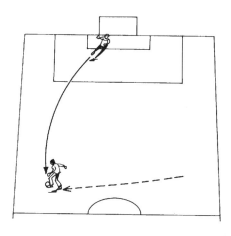

Phase 2

The goalkeeper kicks the ball as quickly as possible into the path of the coach, who is running into space. The coach varies the direction of his runs. If the coach is near the center line or in the other half of the pitch, the goalkeeper can punt or half-volley the ball. If the coach is in the same half as the goalkeeper, the goalkeeper can throw the ball. If the coach is near the penalty area the goalkeeper can roll the ball into his path. The coach controls the ball and runs with it until the goalkeeper has resumed his starting position in goal, and so on.

Participants:	1 goalkeeper	Equipment:	1 ball
	Coach		1 goal
			1 soccer field

Throwing and kicking the ball into play

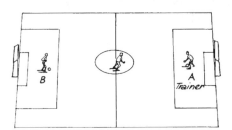

Starting position

The goalkeeper stands in the center circle. The coach (A) is in one penalty area and an outfield player (B) is in the other. They both have a ball at their feet.

Phase 1

The coach kicks the ball out low, high or medium-high to the center circle. The goalkeeper's task is to catch the ball securely before it touches the ground inside the center circle

Phase 2

When the goalkeeper has secured the ball, the coach runs into space on the wing. The goalkeeper half-volleys the ball into the path of the coach, who controls it and runs back into the penalty area with the ball at his feet.

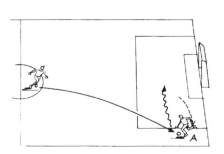

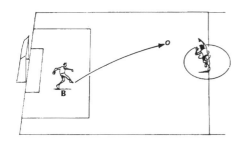

Phase 3

Immediately after half-volleying the ball to the coach, the goalkeeper turns toward the outfield player. The outfield player kicks the ball out and the goalkeeper secures it as described in Phase 1, and so on.

Variations

1. The goalkeeper volleys the ball into the path of the coach instead of half-volleying it.

2. The goalkeeper throws the balls overarm to the coach and the outfield player.

Throwing and kicking the ball into play

Participants:	1 goalkeeper	Equipment:	2 balls
	Coach		2 goals
	1 outfield player		1 soccer field

Throwing and kicking the ball into play

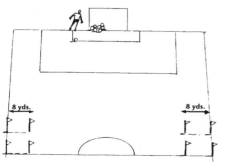

Starting position

The goalkeeper stands to the right of his right-hand post, ready to take a goal kick. Another 7 balls are on the ground in the goalmouth. Two squares with sides 8 yards long are marked at the right and left ends of the center line (4 marker flags per square).

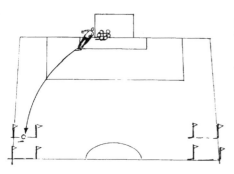

Phase 1

The goalkeeper tries to direct his goal kick so that the ball lands in the square to his right.

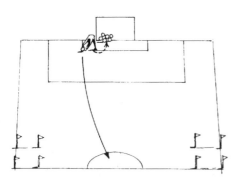

Phase 2

The goalkeeper runs to take the next ball from the goalmouth, places it at the corner of the goal area and takes another goal kick, this time aiming to land the ball in the center circle, and so on. The sequence in which the 3 zones are aimed at can be defined at random (for example, right zone, center circle, left zone, center circle, etc.).

53

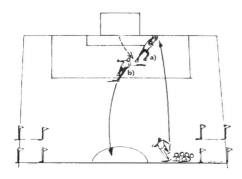

Variations

1. The goalkeeper stands in his goal. The coach stands on the center line with a ball at his feet. The other balls are on the ground nearby. He kicks the ball high in front of goal. The goalkeeper comes off his line and jumps to catch the ball. He then touches the ground with the ball and volleys it into the zone indicated by the coach.

2. The goalkeeper half-volleys the ball into the target zone.

3. The goalkeeper throws the balls overarm into the target zone.

4. The two zones on the right and left are marked out on the side of the center line in the other half of the pitch.

• Throwing and kicking the ball into play

Participants:	1 goalkeeper	Equipment:	8 balls
Variations 1-4:	Coach		1 goal
			1 soccer field
			8 marker flags

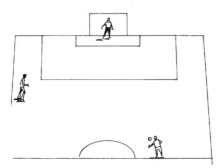

Starting position

The goalkeeper stands in his goal. An outfield player stands to the right of the center circle with a ball 2 yards away from his feet. The coach stands on the left wing, roughly level with the edge of the penalty area.

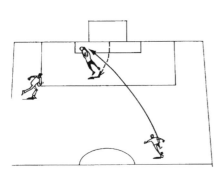

Phase 1

The outfield player runs up and crosses a high ball in front of the goal. The goalkeeper leaves his line and jumps to catch the ball. At the same time the coach moves infield and takes up position on the edge of the penalty area, level with the goalkeeper, ready to receive the ball from the goalkeeper.

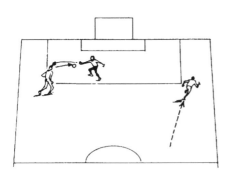

Phase 2

After catching the ball, the goalkeeper throws it as quickly as possible in a high arc to the coach. The coach heads the ball back to the goalkeeper, who catches it. Meanwhile the outfield player has made a run to the right corner of the penalty area.

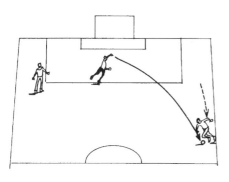

Phase 3

As soon as the coach heads the ball back to the goalkeeper, the outfield player runs back down the wing toward the center line. When the goalkeeper catches the ball he immediately throws into the path of the outfield player. The outfield player must control the ball before he reaches the center line. The outfield player, the goalkeeper and the coach resume their starting positions, and so on.

Variations

In Phase 3 the goalkeeper volleys the ball to the sprinting outfield player. The outfield player runs from midfield, down the wing, into the other half of the pitch.

• Throwing and kicking the ball into play

Participants:	1 goalkeeper	Equipment:	1 ball
	1 outfield player		1 goal
	Coach		1 half of the field
		Variation:	1 soccer field

• Throwing and kicking the ball into play

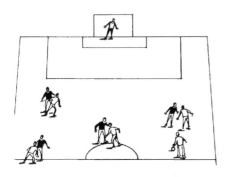

Starting position
The goalkeeper stands in his goal. The coach stands on the center line with a ball at his feet. The outfield players (4 attackers and 4 defenders) stand in pairs in a zone that starts at the edge of the penalty area and stops 20 yards behind the center line.

Phase 1
The coach plays a high ball in front of goal. The goalkeeper leaves his line and jumps to catch the ball.

Phase 2
As soon as the goalkeeper has the ball, the defenders run into space. Their task is to take up positions that give the goalkeeper a number of options for sending the ball back into play. The goalkeeper tries to throw the ball as fast as possible to the defender who has distanced himself best from his attacker. Depending on the situation, the goalkeeper can pass or roll the ball to a defender near the penalty area, throw it to a defender in the middle of the half, or kick it to a defender near the center line.

Phase 3
The defender controls the ball and plays it to the coach. Meanwhile the goalkeeper has run back to his goal, so the coach can send another high ball into the goalmouth, and so on.

Variations
1. The defenders exchange passes before playing the ball back to the coach.
2. The defenders and attackers swap roles after each throw or kick into play.
3. The coach assigns identities to the two groups of four paired outfield players (black/white). When the goalkeeper catches the ball, the coach calls out which group has to run into space.

• **Throwing and kicking the ball into play**

Participants:	1 goalkeeper	Equipment:	1 ball
	8 outfield players		1 goal
	Coach		1 soccer field

Throwing and kicking the ball into play

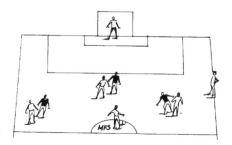

Starting position

The goalkeeper stands in his goal. The outfield players are in midfield. They form 2 teams (4 v 3). 1 midfield player supports 3 attackers, who are marked by 3 defenders. The midfield player has a ball at his feet. The coach stands at the side of the pitch and observes, directs and corrects the events on the pitch.

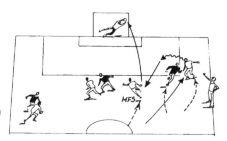

Phase 1

The attacking team tries to score a goal as quickly as possible. The midfield player is only allowed to shoot at goal from outside of the penalty area.

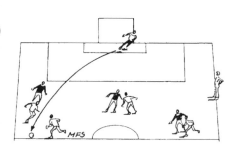

Phase 2

a) If the ball goes out of play or a goal is scored, the attackers and defenders return to the midfield zone and the midfield player takes up a position near the center line. The goalkeeper takes a goal kick, aiming to reach the midfield player, who makes a run into space. The other players try to intercept the ball before it reaches him.

59

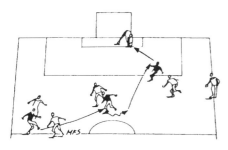

b) If the defenders win the ball, they must pass or head the ball back to the goalkeeper either immediately or after a number of passes. The goalkeeper positions himself at the near post. The attackers try to prevent the ball from reaching the goalkeeper.

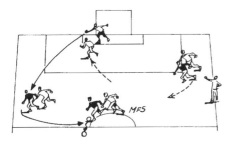

c) If the goalkeeper gains possession from a shot at goal or a backpass, the defenders run into space. The attacker closest to the goalkeeper runs toward the goalkeeper and tries to prevent him from kicking or throwing the ball into play. The other 2 attackers follow their direct opponents and the midfield player immediately moves to cover the unmarked defender. The goalkeeper plays the ball to the defender who gets furthest away from his opponent. If the defenders succeed in interpassing the ball up to the center line and one of them crosses the center line with the ball at his feet, the teams swap tasks. The defenders become attackers and the attackers become defenders.

Variations
If the goalkeeper gains possession from a shot or a backpass (see Phase 2c), all of the attackers try to prevent him from throwing or kicking the ball into play. The goalkeeper has the task of playing the ball to the defender who is furthest from goal. This player controls the ball and passes to the midfield player, who then joins the former defenders in an attack.

• Throwing and kicking the ball into play

Participants:	1 goalkeeper	Equipment:	1 ball
	7 outfield players		1 goal
	Coach		1 half of the field

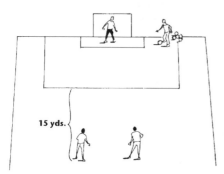

Starting position

The goalkeeper stands in his goal. The coach stands to the side of the goal, between the side of the goal area and the side of the penalty area. He has a ball at his feet. Another 5 balls are on the ground nearby. Two outfield players stand 15 yards in front of the penalty area in line with the right and left goal posts.

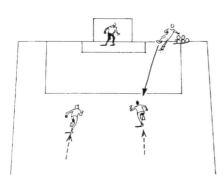

Phase 1

At a call from the coach the 2 outfield players start to run straight toward the goal. As soon as they near the edge of the penalty area, the coach plays the ball into the path of one of them so that he can shoot directly or after a first controlling touch. The coach plays the ball randomly to one player or the other.

• Positional play

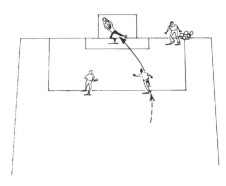

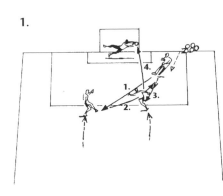

1.

Phase 2

The goalkeeper focuses on the ball and continuously changes position accordingly. He tries to stop the outfield player's shot. If he catches the ball he rolls it back to the coach. At the same time the coach takes the next ball and the outfield players return to their starting positions, and so on.

Variations

1. The first outfield player passes the ball back to the coach, who comes toward the player to meet the return pass. The coach passes low to the other outfield player, who has stopped his forward run at the edge of the penalty area. This outfield player runs to meet the coach's pass and shoots at goal. The goalkeeper focuses on the ball, continuously changing position accordingly.

2. The first outfield player passes along the ground to the second one when he receives the ball from the coach. The second outfield player shoots on the run.

3. Both outfield players try to score if the ball rebounds into play after a shot at goal.

• Positional play

Participants:	1 goalkeeper	Equipment:	6 balls
	2 outfield players		1 goal
	Coach		1 half of the field

Starting position

The goalkeeper stands in his goal. Three outfield players (A, B and C) stand level, 20 yards in front of the penalty area. Player B has a ball at his feet. The coach stands at the corner of the penalty area. He directs and corrects the events on the pitch.

Phase 1

At a call from the coach the 3 outfield players start to run straight toward the goal. Player B runs with the ball at his feet. The players try to stay level.

Positional play

Phase 2

Just before he reaches the penalty area, player B passes diagonally forward into the path of player A. The goalkeeper focuses on the ball and continuously changes position accordingly. Player A shoots on the run. The goalkeeper tries to stop the shot. He can catch the ball, deflect it wide of the goal or punch it away. If he catches the ball, he rolls it to player C. When player C has the ball, all of the players, including the goalkeeper, return to their starting positions, and so on.

Variations

1. Player B hits a surprise shot at the goal.

2. Players A and B run forward at a distance of 5 yards from each other. Each has a ball at his feet. One of them shoots, by prior agreement, from the edge of the penalty area, while the other passes diagonally forward into the path of player C, who runs onto the ball and shoots. After trying to stop the first shot the goalkeeper turns immediately to face player C and tries to stop the second shot.

3. Each of the 3 outfield players tries to score if the ball rebounds into play after a shot at goal.

2.

C · B · A · 5 yds.

● **Positional play**

Participants:	1 goalkeeper	Equipment:	1 ball
	3 outfield players		1 goal
	Coach		1 half of the field
		Variations 2 and 3:	2 balls

64

Starting position

The goalkeeper stands in his goal. The outfield players run around in the zone formed by the front edge of the penalty area and an imaginary parallel line drawn through the penalty spot. Each outfield player has a number. One of them has a ball at his feet. The coach stands at the corner of the penalty area. He observes, directs and corrects the events on the pitch. Another 5 balls are on the ground nearby.

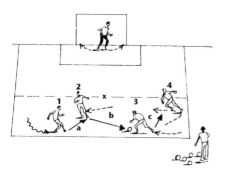

Phase 1

The outfield players remain in motion, passing the ball to each other and continuously changing position. The goalkeeper focuses on the ball and continuously changes position accordingly.

• **Positional play**

65

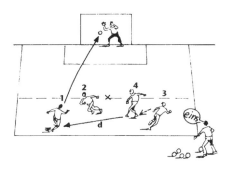

Phase 2

After 4 or 5 passes the coach calls out a number between 1 and 4. As soon as the player with this number receives the ball, he shoots at goal. The goalkeeper tries to stop the shot. If he catches the ball, he throws it to the coach. Meanwhile the coach takes the next ball, passes it to one of the outfield players, and so on.

Variations

1. Each of the outfield players tries to score if the ball rebounds into play after a shot at goal.

2. Each outfield player is assigned a specific part of the goal to shoot at (top right, bottom left, etc.) This is agreed before the start of the drill without the goalkeeper's knowledge.

3. The players take surprise shots at goal after 2 or 3 passes, without any prior call from the coach.

• Positional play

Participants:	1 goalkeeper	Equipment:	6 balls
	4 outfield players		1 goal
	Coach		penalty area

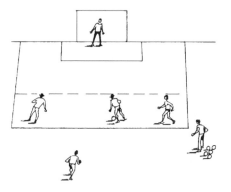

Starting position

The goalkeeper stands in his goal. Three outfield players run around in the zone formed by the front edge of the penalty area and an imaginary parallel line drawn through the penalty spot. One of them has a ball at his feet. A fourth outfield player stands 30 yards in front of the goal. The coach stands at the corner of the penalty area. He observes, directs and corrects the events on the pitch. Another 5 balls are on the ground nearby.

Phase 1

The 3 outfield players remain in motion, passing the ball to each other. The passer always chases behind his pass. The goalkeeper focuses on the ball and continuously changes position accordingly. After a few passes the ball is suddenly laid back to the outfield player positioned outside of the penalty area.

Positional play

67

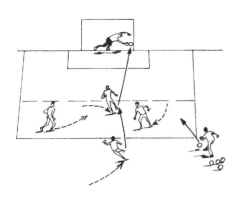

Phase 2

The player outside the penalty area runs onto the ball and shoots directly at goal. The 3 players in the penalty area obscure the goalkeeper's line of vision and try to deflect the ball as it flies past them, so that the goalkeeper will have to quickly adjust his initial movement. After each shot the marksman swaps places with one of the 3 players in the penalty area. The goalkeeper tries to stop the shot. If he catches the ball, he throws it to the coach. Meanwhile the coach takes the next ball, passes it to one of the outfield players in the penalty area, and so on.

Variations

1. Each of the outfield players tries to score if the ball rebounds into play after a shot at goal.
2. The players in the penalty area take surprise shots at goal rather than laying the ball back for the fourth player.

• Positional play

Participants: 1 goalkeeper	**Equipment:** 6 balls
4 outfield players	1 goal
Coach	penalty area

Starting position

The goalkeeper stands in his goal. Four outfield players are about 10 yards in front of the penalty area. Each outfield player has a ball at his feet. The coach stands at the corner of the penalty area. He observes, directs and corrects the events on the pitch.

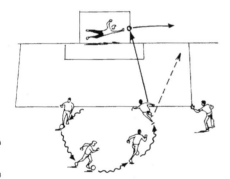

Phase 1

The outfield players run in single file in a large circle, each with a ball at his feet. The coach tells the first player which path to take. The goalkeeper focuses on this path and continuously changes position accordingly. This player runs into the penalty area and shoots on the run. The goalkeeper tries to stop the shot. If he catches it, he throws it back to the marksman, who joins the back of the line of players.

• **Positional play**

Phase 2

After each shot the goalkeeper immediately focuses on the next player and
continuously changes position accordingly. This player runs into the penalty
area from a different angle and shoots
at goal, and so on. The outfield players must continuously vary the angle
of their runs into the penalty area,
shooting from right, left, the middle,
on the turn, etc.

Variation

The outfield players run along the
edge of the penalty area, constantly
changing positions. Each outfield
player is assigned a number. The
coach calls out a number and the cor-
responding player immediately shoots
at goal while on the move.

• Positional play

Participants: 1 goalkeeper	**Equipment:** 4 balls
4 outfield players	1 goal
Coach	penalty area

Key aspects

- Coming to meet an advancing attacker
- Winning the ball

- Diving to stop low balls
- Reaction speed
- Deflecting the ball
- Defending with the feet
- Speed off the mark

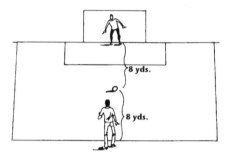

Starting position

The goalkeeper stands in his goal. The coach stands directly in front of the goal at the edge of the penalty area. The ball lies between the goalkeeper and the coach about 8 yards from the goal.

Phase 1

At a call from the coach, the goalkeeper and the coach race toward the ball.

• One against one

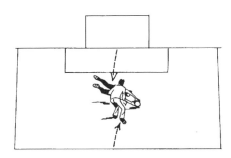

Phase 2

The goalkeeper throws himself to the ground at the coach's feet, with his body behind the ball and across the line of the coach's run. If he reaches the ball before the coach, he clutches it to his body with both hands. If the coach reaches the ball first, the goalkeeper's body forms the widest possible obstacle. The coach tries to slide the ball wide of the goalkeeper's body or chip it over him into the goal. The goalkeeper must try to prevent this with his feet or hands. The ball is replaced and the coach and the goalkeeper resume their starting positions, and so on.

Variations

1. The coach starts further to the side, so that he is no longer directly in front of the goalkeeper. He runs diagonally toward the ball. The coach must take care to stand at the same distance as the goalkeeper from the ball.

2. The coach stands directly in front of the goalkeeper as before, but the ball is placed to one side.

• One against one

Participants: 1 goalkeeper Coach	Equipment: 1 ball 1 goal penalty area

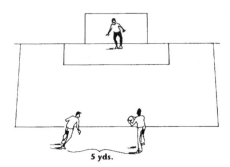

Starting position
The goalkeeper stands in his goal. The outfield player stands outside the penalty area. The coach, who is standing 5 yards to the right of the outfield player, holds a ball.

Phase 1
The coach calls out and then throws the ball into the free space between the goalkeeper and the outfield player. Both race toward the ball. The outfield player varies his starting position, so that he can start his run from various directions and distances. The coach throws the ball closer to the goalkeeper or the outfield player at random. Depending on the starting position of the outfield player, the coach can also throw the ball so that the goalkeeper has to run out of the penalty area.

• **One against one**

Phase 2

Depending on the situation, the goalkeeper kicks the ball away from inside or outside of the penalty area, picks the ball up inside the penalty area or dives at the outfield player's feet to grasp the ball to his body or deflect it to the side with his hand or foot. The outfield player's task is to dribble the ball past the goalkeeper or to lob it over his head or slide it past him into the goal. The goalkeeper can throw the ball to the coach or the outfield player may have to fetch the ball and throw it to the coach. As soon as the goalkeeper and the outfield player have resumed their starting positions the coach throws the ball again, and so on.

• One against one

Participants: 1 goalkeeper	**Equipment:** 1 ball
1 outfield player	
Coach	

Starting position

The goalkeeper stands in his goal. The outfield player stands 5 yards in front of the center circle. The coach stands 5 yards to the right of the center circle on the center line. He is holding a ball and 5 other balls are on the ground nearby.

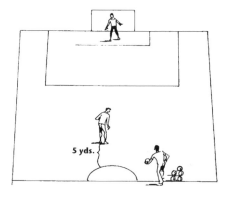

5 yds.

Phase 1

The coach kicks a ball in the direction of the goal. It can be low or medium-high or can bounce between the outfield player and the goal.

• One against one

75

Phase 2

When the coach kicks the ball the goalkeeper and the outfield player race to meet it. The goalkeeper tries to get there first and kick the ball away to the side or straight ahead. If the attacker is very close the goalkeeper kicks the ball to the side to avoid any risk of it hitting the attacker. At first the coach gives the goalkeeper the advantage, so that he can kick the ball away while inside the penalty area. The coach then kicks the ball in such a way that the goalkeeper has to run out of his penalty area to kick the ball away. The goalkeeper and the outfield player then resume their starting positions, the coach kicks the next ball forward, and so on.

Variations

1. The coach plays the ball to the right or left side of the penalty area.

2. The coach stands behind the outfield player and plays the ball diagonally past him or over him in the direction of the penalty area.

• One against one

Participants:	1 goalkeeper	Equipment:	6 balls
	1 outfield player		1 goal
	Coach		1 half of the field

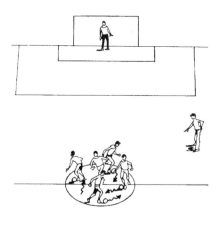

Starting position
The goalkeeper stands in his goal. The outfield players jog around in the center circle. Each has a ball at his feet. The coach stands to the right near the corner of the penalty area. He observes, directs and controls the events on the pitch.

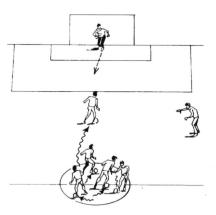

Phase 1
At a call from the coach, one outfield player runs from the center circle toward the goal with a ball at his feet. He can approach the penalty area from the left or right or through the middle. When he is midway between the goal and the center line, the goalkeeper comes off his line and moves out to meet the approaching outfield player.

• One against one

Phase 2

The goalkeeper tries to confront the outfield player as far away from the goal as possible in the penalty area. He must not hesitate when he leaves the goal. He narrows the angle and watches the ball and the foot with which the player will shoot. When he is close to the outfield player, the goalkeeper stops and crouches. When the outfield player tries to dribble past him, he tries to block, clasp or deflect the ball with his feet, body or hands, if necessary by diving at the outfield player's feet. The outfield player subsequently fetches the ball and runs back to the center line with the ball at his feet. The goalkeeper sprints back to his goal, the coach calls out, and the next player starts his run at goal, and so on.

Variation

Just before the goalkeeper reaches him, the outfield player tries to push the ball past him or lob it over him.

• One against one

Participants:	1 goalkeeper	**Equipment:**	5 balls
	5 outfield players		1 goal
	Coach		1 center circle

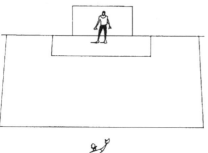

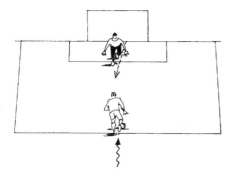

Starting position

The goalkeeper stands in his goal. The coach stands outside the penalty area with a ball at his feet.

Phase 1

The coach makes a straight or diagonal forward run with the ball under close control. The goalkeeper comes off his line and narrows the angle, watching the ball and the foot with which the coach will shoot. Just before he reaches the coach, the goalkeeper stops moving forward and crouches.

Phase 2

The coach tries to dribble past the goalkeeper, while still giving him a chance to get to the ball. The goalkeeper dives at the coach's feet. He clasps the ball to his body or deflects the ball to the side with his hands or feet. The goalkeeper then runs back to his goal, while the coach fetches the ball and runs away from the goal with the ball at his feet. He then makes a run at the goal from another direction, and so on.

Variation

When the goalkeeper dives at his feet, the coach tries to push the ball past him or lob it over him.

One against one

| Participants: | 1 goalkeeper Coach | Equipment: | 1 ball 1 goal penalty area |

Key aspects
- Dominating the penalty area
- Coming off the goal line at the right moment
- Winning the ball

- Take-off strength (one-footed running take-off)
- Catching the ball securely

Variation
- One-fisted punching
- Two-fisted punching

Starting position
The goalkeeper stands in his goal. The coach stands beside the penalty spot and holds a ball.

Phase 1
The coach lobs the ball into the air so that it falls toward the edge of the goal. The coach runs behind the ball and the goalkeeper comes off his line.

Phase 2
The goalkeeper jumps to catch the ball. His task is to catch the ball securely in both hands and clasp it to his body while under challenge from the coach, who also jumps and tries to hinder the goalkeeper. The goalkeeper throws the ball back to the coach and they both resume their starting positions, and so on.

Variation
The coach has 6 balls. He throws them in sequence and the goalkeeper punches them away with one or both fists. The coach can specify the direction in which the goalkeeper has to punch the ball.

• Dominating the penalty area

Participants: 1 goalkeeper	**Equipment:**	1 ball
Coach		1 goal
		1 goal area
	Variation:	6 balls

Key aspects
- Dominating the penalty area
- Coming off the goal line at the right moment
- Winning the ball
- Take-off strength (one-footed running take-off)
- Catching the ball securely
- One-fisted punching
- Two-fisted punching

Starting position
The goalkeeper stands in his goal. The outfield player stands between the goal and the penalty spot. The coach stands at the corner of the penalty spot and holds a ball. Another 7 balls lie on the ground nearby.

Phase 1
The coach lobs the ball high into the air so that it falls toward the near or far post or the center of the goal.

Phase 2

The goalkeeper and the outfield player jump to the ball. Depending on the situation, the goalkeeper catches or punches the ball. The outfield player impedes the goalkeeper and tries to head the ball into the goal. If the goalkeeper catches the ball he throws it back to the coach. The players resume their starting positions and the coach throws the next ball, and so on.

Variations

1. The coach throws the ball from one of the corners of the penalty area or from the center of the front edge of the penalty area.

2. The coach stands outside the penalty area and crosses the ball from various positions with differing power or swerve.

3. Three outfield players take up different positions in front of the goal and challenge for the ball, impeding the goalkeeper and trying to head the ball into the goal.

• **Dominating the penalty area**

Participants:	1 goalkeeper	**Equipment:**	8 balls
	1 outfield player		1 goal
	Coach		penalty area
Variation 3:	3 outfield players		

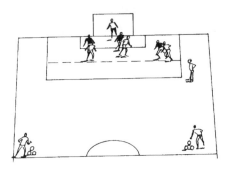

Starting position

The goalkeeper stands in his goal. Three pairs of players (attacker/defender) line up between the goal and a line drawn through the penalty spot and parallel to the goal line. One midfield player stands at each end of the center line. Three balls are on the ground near each midfield player. The coach stands at the right corner of the penalty spot. He observes, directs and corrects the events on the pitch.

Phase 1

The right midfielder crosses a high ball that drops between the goal and the penalty area. Depending on the situation, the goalkeeper catches the ball or punches it under pressure from the attackers. The goalkeeper must challenge for the high ball decisively. The attackers try to impede the goalkeeper and head the ball into the goal. The defenders remain largely passive, jumping toward the ball but without trying to reach it.

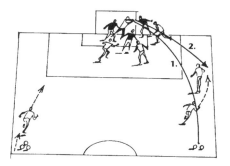

Phase 2

a) If the goalkeeper catches the cross or an attacker's header, the defenders run into space outside the penalty area. The goalkeeper throws the ball to the defender who has escaped from his opponent most successfully. The defender controls the ball and tries to hit a long high pass to the left midfielder, who has also run into space.

b) If the goalkeeper punches the ball, he tries to direct it to one of the midfield players, who have run forward into space outside the penalty area.

Phase 3

As soon as the goalkeeper and the pairs of players have resumed their starting positions, the left midfielder crosses a high ball in front of goal, and so on.

Variations

1. After two crosses, the players making up the pairs swap roles.

2. The pairs of players take up positions between the goal line and the edge of the penalty area. The midfield players cross the ball so that it falls about 12 yards in front of the goal. The goalkeeper must leave his line quickly and decisively to defend his goal against the cross. The attackers try to impede him.

Dominating the penalty area

Participants:	1 goalkeeper	Equipment:	6 balls
	8 outfield player		1 goal
	Coach		1 half of the field

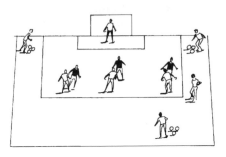

Starting position

The goalkeeper stands in his goal. Three pairs of players (attacker/defender) are in the penalty area. At each corner flag is a corner-taker. In midfield, outside the penalty area, is a midfield player. Three balls are on the ground near the midfield player and each of the 2 corner-takers. The coach stands at the right corner of the penalty spot. He observes, directs and corrects the events on the pitch.

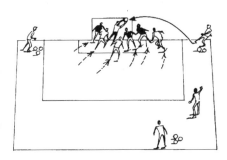

Phase 1

The player on the right hits a high corner kick between the goal and the penalty spot. Depending on the situation, the goalkeeper must catch the ball or punch it. He must challenge for the high ball decisively while under pressure from the attackers. The defenders remain largely passive, jumping toward the ball but without trying to reach it. The attackers try to score with a header or a shot.

• **Dominating the penalty area**

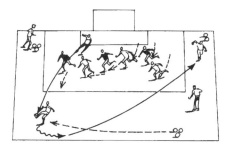

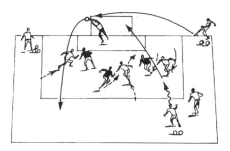

Phase 2

a) If the goalkeeper catches the cross or an attacker's header or shot, he throws or kicks the ball as quickly as possible to the midfield player, who is running across the pitch. The attackers try to impede the goalkeeper when he throws or kicks the ball. The midfielder controls the ball, runs a few steps with it and plays a long diagonal pass to the corner-taker, who is moving slightly infield, away from the corner flag.

b) If the goalkeeper punches the ball, the midfield player makes a forward run and shoots at goal as soon as the goalkeeper is on his feet. The 3 pairs of players continuously change position in front of the goal to impede the goalkeeper's line of vision. If the goalkeeper catches the shot, he plays the ball to the midfield player as described under a).

Phase 3

As soon as the goalkeeper and the pairs of players have resumed their starting positions, a corner kick is taken from the left side of the pitch, and so on.

Variations

1. After one corner from the right and one from the left, the players making up the pairs swap roles.

2. The players taking the corner kicks cross the ball to the near post, the far post or the penalty area in a sequence defined by the coach.

3. The corners from the left are taken with the right foot and the corners from the right with the left foot.

• Dominating the penalty area

Participants:	1 goalkeeper	Equipment:	9 balls
	9 outfield players		1 goal
	Coach		1 half of the field

Key aspects
- One-fisted punching
- Catching technique

Variations 4 to 7
- Take-off strength
- Speed off the mark

Variation 7
- Winning the ball

Starting position

The swingball hangs at shoulder height about 2 feet from the goalkeeper, who stands in the stride position with one foot forward and one back and one shoulder toward the ball. The arm furthest away from the ball is drawn back with the elbow bent, touching his side.

Phase 1

The goalkeeper straightens his arm and punches the ball centrally. As he punches, his upper body turns so that the shoulder of the punching arm is closest to the ball. As he punches the ball, the back of his hand is facing up.

Phase 2

The goalkeeper catches the ball with both hands as it swings back. The goalkeeper resumes his starting position in front of the suspended ball, and so on.

• Swingball

3.

5.

6.

Variations

1. The goalkeeper punches the swinging ball at its lowest point of its path as it swings back to him.

2. The goalkeeper punches the swinging ball with his left and right fist alternately.

3. The suspended ball hangs above the goalkeeper but within his reach. His shoulders are aligned in the direction of the ball's swing. The goalkeeper punches the swinging or motionlessly suspended ball from the side.

4. The goalkeeper makes a 2-footed take-off and punches the swinging or motionlessly suspended ball from the side.

5. The goalkeeper takes a short run and makes a 1-footed take-off, punching the swinging or motionlessly suspended ball from the side.

6. The goalkeeper stands under the arc of the swinging ball. He makes a 2-footed take-off and punches the ball behind him with one fist. He punches the ball from the side and below when it is exactly above his body.

7. An outfield player impedes the goalkeeper as he jumps (variations 4 to 6).

• **Swingball**

Participants: 1 goalkeeper   **Equipment:**   1 swingball
Variation 7:   1 outfield player

Starting position

The swingball hangs at shoulder height about 2 feet from the goalkeeper, who stands with his legs apart to the right and left. He holds his fists in front of his chest and his bent elbows are held close to his body.

Phase 1

The goalkeeper straightens his arms explosively and punches the ball centrally with both fists.

Phase 2

The goalkeeper catches the ball with both hands as it swings back and allows it to hang motionless. The goalkeeper resumes his starting position in front of the suspended ball, and so on.

• **Swingball**

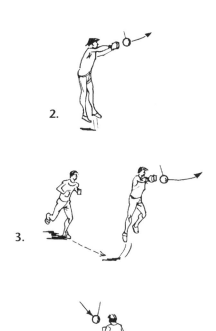

Variations

1. The goalkeeper punches the swinging ball at the lowest point of its path as it swings back to him.

2. The suspended ball hangs within jumping reach. The goalkeeper makes a 2-footed standing take-off and punches the motionlessly suspended or the swinging ball. He can hop once to gain momentum before he jumps to punch the ball again.

3. The goalkeeper stands 5 yards from the suspended ball. He takes a running 2-footed jump and punches the ball.

4. After the goalkeeper has taken a running one-footed jump and punched the ball, he continues his run to the other side and then turns back toward the suspended ball. In the meantime the ball has swung back and forth so that the goalkeeper can jump to punch it again.

5. An outfield player stands under the ball and impedes the goalkeeper as he jumps (variations 2 to 4).

• **Swingball**

| **Participants:** 1 goalkeeper | **Equipment:** 1 swingball |
| **Variation 5:** 1 outfield player | |

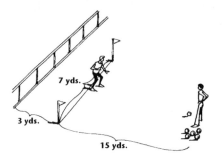

Starting position

A goal is formed parallel to the railing by placing 2 marker flags 6 yards apart. The goalkeeper stands between the flags, facing the coach, who is 15 yards away and has a ball at his feet. Another 5 balls lie nearby.

Phase 1

At a call from the coach, the goalkeeper sprints to the railing and vaults over it.

Phase 2

After landing the goalkeeper crawls back under the railing and sprints back to the goal line.

• Railing

Phase 3

As soon as the goalkeeper is back in his goal, the coach shoots hard and low, high or medium-high at the goal. The goalkeeper must try to catch the ball securely in both hands. He then throws it back to the coach. The coach then calls again, and so on.

Variations

The goalkeeper jumps over the railing twice in succession. As he sprints back to the goal line he jumps to catch the ball, which the coach has thrown in a high arc toward the goal.

• Railing

Participants:	1 goalkeeper	Equipment:	6 balls
	Coach		Railing
			2 marker flags

Key aspects
- Agility
- Take-off strength
- Speed off the mark
- Diving to stop low balls
- Diving to stop high to medium-high balls

- Reaction speed
- Catching the ball securely
- Punching the ball
- Deflecting the ball

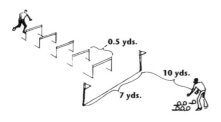

0.5 yds.

10 yds.

7 yds.

Starting position

Between 5 and 7 hurdles are arranged lined up in parallel at intervals of about 2 feet. A 7-yard wide goal is formed by 2 marker flags about 3 yards from the first hurdle. The goalkeeper stands behind the final hurdle. The coach stands about 10 yards in front of the goal.

Phase 1

The goalkeeper sprints over all the hurdles. He can take an extra step between hurdles if necessary.

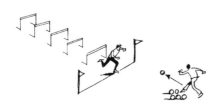

Phase 2

After jumping over the last hurdle the goalkeeper sprints to the goal. At the same time the coach shoots powerfully at the goal. He varies the height and direction of the shot.

· Hurdles, marker flags

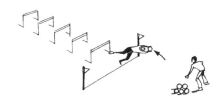

Phase 3

The sprinting goalkeeper dives forward to stop the ball from crossing the goal line. He can catch the ball, punch it away or deflect it to the side. If he catches it, he rolls it back to the coach. The goalkeeper then trots back to his starting position, and so on.

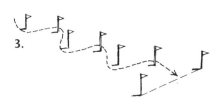

1.

Variations

1. The goalkeeper crawls under one hurdle, jumps over the next, etc.

2. The goalkeeper slaloms through the line of hurdles.

3. The goalkeeper slaloms through 6 marker flags positioned in a zigzag line at short intervals from each other.

4. The coach drops the ball and half-volleys it.

5. As goalkeeper A trots back to the first hurdle, goalkeeper B sprints over the hurdles, and so on.

3.

• **Hurdles, marker flags**

Participants:	1 goalkeeper	**Equipment:**	6 balls
	Coach		5 - 7 hurdles
Variation 5:	2 goalkeepers		2 marker flags
		Variation 3:	8 marker flags

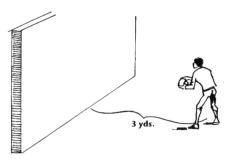

Starting position

The goalkeeper stands 3 yards from the wall. He is holding a ball.

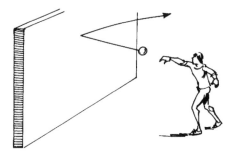

Phase 1

The goalkeeper throws the ball power-fully at the wall.

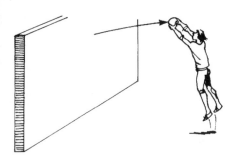

Phase 2

The goalkeeper jumps to catch the rebound securely in both hands. He must position his fingers correctly.

• Shooting wall

Variations

1. The goalkeeper throws the ball at random at different heights. He catches the rebound securely in both hands. He must position his fingers correctly.

2. The goalkeeper bounces the ball against the wall.

3. The goalkeeper stands 4 yards away from the ball. He drops the ball and volleys it against the wall.

4. The goalkeeper waits until the rebound is behind him, then turns quickly, dives after the ball and catches it.

5. After throwing the ball, the goalkeeper makes a complete clockwise or counterclockwise turn.

6. After throwing the ball, the goalkeeper squats or sits, falls into the press-up position, lies on his front or back or performs a forward roll. He then leaps to his feet and catches the ball.

● Shooting wall

Participant: 1 goalkeeper	Equipment: 1 ball
	1 wall

Shooting wall

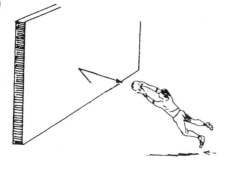

Starting position

The goalkeeper stands 8 yards from the wall. He is holding a ball.

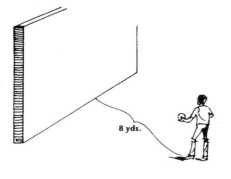

Phase 1

The goalkeeper drops the ball and volleys it powerfully at the wall.

Phase 2

The goalkeeper immediately runs after the ball and dives forward or to the side to catch it He must focus on his catching technique.

8 yds.

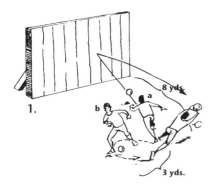

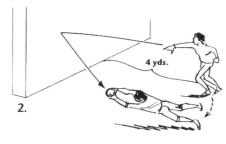

1.

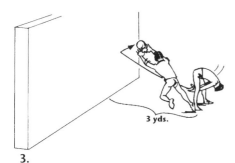

2.

3.

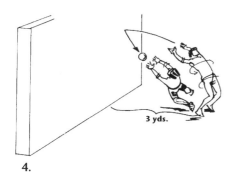

4.

Variations

1. The goalkeeper stands 8 yards from the wall, holding a ball. Another ball is on the ground 3 yards to his left or behind him. The goalkeeper drops the ball he is holding and volleys it powerfully at the wall. He then runs round the other ball or touches it with his hand or dives on it and clutches it to his body. He then runs toward the rebound and dives to catch it.

2. The goalkeeper throws the ball diagonally against the wall from a distance of 4 yards. He then runs and dives to catch the rebound.

3. The goalkeeper stands 3 yards away from the wall with his back to it. His legs are apart. He bends and throws the ball through his legs against the wall. He quickly makes a half turn (clockwise or counterclockwise) and catches the rebound.

4. The goalkeeper stands 3 yards away from the wall with his back to it. He throws the ball over his head, either straight back or slightly to the side, against the wall.

5. The goalkeeper sidefoots the ball against the wall from a distance of 3 yards. He moves toward the rebound, allows the ball to pass between his legs, makes a half turns (clockwise or counterclockwise) and then dives onto the ball and clutches it to his body.

6. The goalkeeper moves closer to the wall in one-yard steps, so that he has to react more quickly.

7. The goalkeeper stands 1 or 2 yards from the wall. He punches the ball against the wall with both fists and with the right and left fist alternately.

• Shooting wall

Participant:	1 goalkeeper	Equipment:	1 ball
			1 wall
		Variation 1:	2 balls

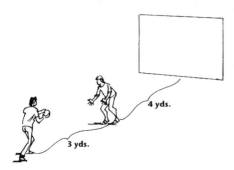

Starting position

The goalkeeper stands 4 yards from the wall with his back to it, facing the coach, who is 3 yards away. The coach is holding a ball.

Phase 1

The coach throws the ball low, high or medium-high to the goalkeeper.

Phase 2

The goalkeeper catches the ball and throws it back to the coach at waist or chest height. He then turns clockwise or counterclockwise to face the wall. At the same moment the coach throws the ball over or past the goalkeeper against the wall.

• Shooting wall

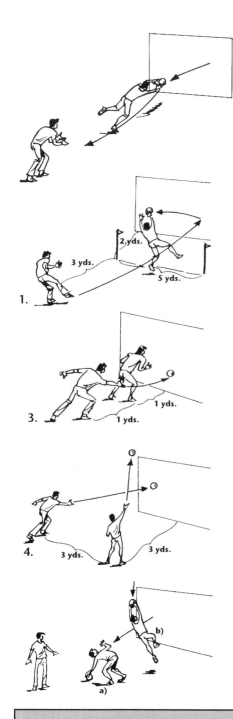

Phase 3

The goalkeeper catches the rebound, diving if necessary. He resumes his starting position and throws the ball back to the coach, and so on.

Variations

1. The goalkeeper stands 2 yards from the wall, facing it. The coach stands 3 yards behind him, holding a ball. One yard behind the goalkeeper are 2 marker flags, which form a goal 5 yards wide. The coach shoots at various heights past the goalkeeper, or over his head, against the wall. The goalkeeper caches the rebound before it crosses the goal line.

2. The goalkeeper faces the coach and carries out alternate clockwise and counterclockwise turns.

3. The goalkeeper faces the wall from a distance of 1 yard. The coach stands 1 yard behind him and throws the ball past or over the goalkeeper, who tries to catch the rebound with both hands.

4. The goalkeeper stands 3 yards away from the wall. The coach stands 3 yards to the side of the goalkeeper. Both are holding a ball. The coach throws his ball against the wall. At the same time the goalkeeper launches his ball vertically into the air. The goalkeeper catches the rebound, places the ball on the ground and dives to catch his own ball. He must try to catch it before it bounces twice.

• Shooting wall

Participants:	1 goalkeeper	Equipment:	1 ball
	Coach		1 wall
		Variation 1:	2 marker flags
		Variation 4:	2 balls

Diving to stop a powerful shot at goal requires a lot of skill. The basics elements of goalkeeping such as diving, take-off strength, agility, catching technique and catching the ball securely must be repeatedly practiced.

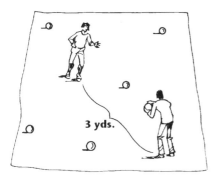

Starting position
The goalkeeper and the coach stand in a sandpit measuring 5 x 5 yards. The coach faces the goalkeeper at a distance of 3 yards. He is holding a ball. Another 5 balls are distributed around the sandpit.

Phase 1
The coach throws the ball high or medium-high to the left or right of the goalkeeper. The goalkeeper dives and catches the ball in both hands. When the coach throws the ball he must take care that the goalkeeper will not land on one of the other balls.

Phase 2
After landing the goalkeeper leaves the ball on the ground and springs to his feet. At the same time the coach runs to the nearest ball, picks it up and throws it to one side of the goalkeeper, and so on.

• Sandpit

Participants: 1 goalkeeper
Coach

Equipment: 6 balls
1 sandpit

Tips for carrying out drills that involve diving over tires:

- The number of tires that are stacked or laid next to each other depends on the level of skill of the goalkeeper.
- The coach must always stand on the side of the tires to which the goalkeeper dives. He is then in a better position to throw the ball so that the goalkeeper can reach it and catch it with both hands.
- The coach must throw the ball immediately after the goalkeeper springs to his feet, for example after a forward roll.
- The coach must throw the ball high enough, as the tires force the goalkeeper to dive upward.

Key aspects
- Agility
- Diving to stop high to medium-high balls
- Take-off strength
- Reaction speed
- Catching the ball securely
- Lower arm extensors

- Shoulder muscles

Variations 1 - 3
- Leg extensors

Variations 1 and 2
- Abdominal muscles
- Hip flexors

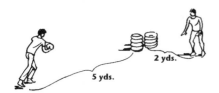

Starting position
The goalkeeper stands 2 yards to the right of 2 stacks of tires placed next to each other. The coach is about 5 yards away from the tires. He is holding a ball.

Phase 1
The goalkeeper performs press-ups.

Phase 2
At a call from the coach, the goalkeeper springs to his feet and faces the coach. As soon as the goalkeeper is on his feet, the coach throws the ball high to the left of the tires.

Tires

Phase 3

The goalkeeper dives over the tires immediately or takes one step toward the tires and then dives.

Phase 4

The goalkeeper catches the ball with both hands. On landing he throws the ball back to the coach, runs back to his starting position and starts performing press-ups, and so on.

Variations

1. Instead of press-ups, the goalkeeper can perform jumps from a squatting position, either straightening his legs or keeping them bent, or lie on his back and raise and lower his legs and upper body (jack-knife), etc.

2. The goalkeeper stands to the left of the tires and the coach throws the ball up to the right.

3. The goalkeeper dives alternately right and left over the tires. After each landing he squats, jumps upward and takes a short step to gain sufficient momentum for the next dive. The coach switches his position continuously so that he is always on the side to which the goalkeeper dives.

• **Tires**

Participants: 1 goalkeeper Coach	**Equipment:** 1 ball 6-14 tires

Key aspects
- Agility
- Diving to stop low balls
- Diving to stop high to medium-high balls
- Take-off strength
- Reaction speed
- Catching the ball securely

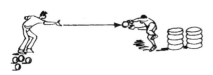

Starting position

The goalkeeper stands 5 yards away from the coach. Immediately behind the goalkeeper are 2 stacks of tires. The coach stands slightly to the right of an imaginary extended line drawn through the tires and is holding a ball. Another 4 balls are nearby.

Phase 1

The coach throws the ball low, 2 or 3 yards to the right of the goalkeeper. From his standing position the goalkeeper dives toward the ball.

Phase 2

The goalkeeper catches the ball with both hands. At the same time the coach picks up the next ball.

• Tires

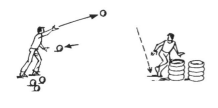

Phase 3

While still on the ground the goal-keeper throws the ball back to the coach, then springs to his feet and runs back to the tires. As soon as the goalkeeper is 2 yards from the tires the coach throws the second ball up 1 or 2 yards to the right of the tires.

Phase 4

The goalkeeper takes a running dive over the tires and catches the ball in both hands. After landing he throws the ball back to the coach, takes up his starting position in front of the tires, and so on.

Variation

The coach throws the first ball low to the goalkeeper's left, the second high to the right of the tires, and so on.

• Tires

| **Participants:** 1 goalkeeper | **Equipment:** 5 balls |
| Coach | 6-14 tires |

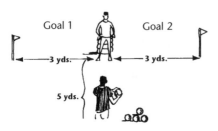

Starting position

The goalkeeper stands 5 yards away from the coach with his back to him. He supports himself with both hands on the first of 2 stacks of tires arranged next to each other. Marker flags are positioned 3 yards to the right and left of the tires, forming 2 goals (1 goal to the goalkeeper's right and one to his left). The coach stands exactly in line with the 2 stacks of tires. He is holding a ball and another 4 balls lie nearby.

Phase 1

The goalkeeper performs press-ups, pushing down on the tires with his full body weight.

Phase 2

The coach calls out to the goalkeeper to tell him where he is going to throw the ball. If the coach indicates goal 1, the goalkeeper turns to his right and runs in a circle round the tires, and for goal 2 he turns to his left and runs round them.

• **Tires**

107

Phase 3

While the goalkeeper is running round the tires, the coach moves to the side to stand in front of the goal he indicated. When the goalkeeper is halfway round the tires the coach throws the ball high to medium-high at the indicated goal.

Phase 4

The goalkeeper takes a running dive over the tires and either catches the ball with both hands, deflects it to the side or punches it away. If he catches the ball he throws back to the coach. The goalkeeper runs back to his starting position and starts to perform press-ups again. The coach picks up the next ball and resumes his starting position, and so on.

Variations

1. The coach calls but does not indicate a goal. If the goalkeeper turns to his right and sprints round the tires, the coach can throw the ball low at goal 2 or high to medium-high at goal 1. If the goalkeeper turns to his left and sprints round the tires, the coach can throw the ball low at goal 1 or high to medium-high at goal 2. While on the run the goalkeeper must immediately dive low or over the tires to stop the ball.

2. The coach stands 15 yards away from the tires and shoots low at goal 1 or high to medium-high at goal 2, or vice versa.

• Tires

Participants: 1 goalkeeper Coach	**Equipment:** 5 balls 6 - 14 tires 2 marker flags

Key aspects
- Agility
- Diving to stop high to medium-high balls
- Take-off strength
- Reaction speed
- Catching the ball securely

Variations
- Punching the ball
- Deflecting the ball

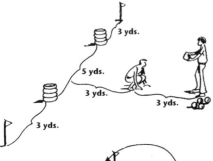

Starting position
Two stacks of tires form a goal 5 yards wide. The goalkeeper squats 3 yards in front of this goal with his back to it. Marker flags are positioned 3 yards to each side of the goal. The coach stands facing the goalkeeper from a distance of 3 yards. He is holding a ball and another 4 balls lie on the ground nearby.

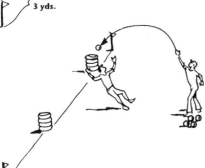

Phase 1
The coach throws the ball in a high arc so that falls behind the goalkeeper. The squatting goalkeeper launches himself backward.

Phase 2
The goalkeeper catches the ball in both hands and rolls it back to the coach, who has meanwhile picked up the next ball.

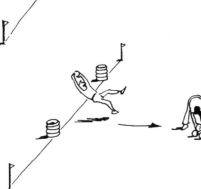

Phase 3
The goalkeeper resumes his starting position and the coach immediately moves to one side and throws the ball high to medium-high, 1 or 2 yards outside the left or right stack of tires.

• Tires

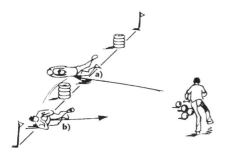

Phase 4

The goalkeeper dives over the stack of tires and catches the ball with both hands. He rolls it back to the coach, who has meanwhile picked up the next ball.

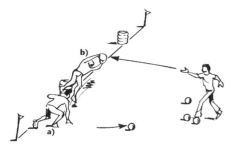

Phase 5

As the goalkeeper springs to his feet, the coach throws the ball high to medium-high, 1 or 2 yards inside the left or right stack of tires. The goalkeeper takes a step toward the tires and dives over the stack toward the ball.

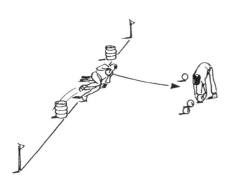

Phase 6

The goalkeeper catches the ball with both hands and rolls it back to the coach. As the coach picks up the next ball the goalkeeper resumes his starting position 3 yards in front of the goal, and so on.

Variation

The coach throws the ball high to medium-high so close to the marker flags that the goalkeeper can only deflect it to the side or punch it away.

• **Tires**

Participants: 1 goalkeeper	Equipment: 5 balls
Coach	6 - 14 tires
	2 marker flags

Key aspects
- Agility
- Diving to stop low balls
- Take-off strength

Variations 1 and 2
- Shoulder muscles

Variation 3
- Leg extensors

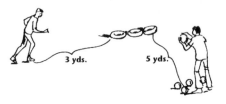

Starting position
The goalkeeper stands in line with and 3 yards away from 3 tires lying next to each other in a line. The coach stands about 5 yards to the right of the tires. He is holding a ball and another 4 balls are on the ground nearby.

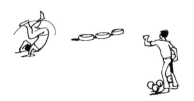

Phase 1
At a call from the coach, the goalkeeper performs a forward roll.

Phase 2
When he finishes his forward roll the goalkeeper is next to the tires. He looks at the coach. At the same time the coach rolls a ball 2 or 3 yards to the right of the tires.

• **Tires**

Phase 3

The goalkeeper dives over the stack of tires, either from a standing position or after taking one pace forward, and catches the ball with both hands. He must try to avoid touching the tires when he lands. While he is still on the ground he rolls the ball back to the coach, then he sprints back to his starting position, and so on.

Variations

1. Instead of a forward roll, the goalkeeper can perform a backward roll and then turn to face the tires, or perform press-ups, etc.

2. The goalkeeper starts by standing on the other side of the tires and the coach throws the ball to the left of the tires.

3. The goalkeeper dives alternately left and right over the tires. After each dive he squats down, leaps up, straightening his legs, and takes one pace to give himself enough momentum for the next dive. The coach stands facing the middle tire.

3.

• **Tires**

Participants: 1 goalkeeper	Equipment:	5 balls
Coach		2-4 tires

- Agility
- Diving to stop high to medium-high balls
- Take-off strength
- Reaction speed

- 2-fisted punching
- 1-fisted punching

Variation 1
- Lower arm extensors
- Shoulder muscles

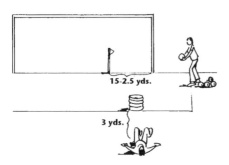

15-2.5 yds.

3 yds.

Starting position

A marker flag is placed 2 yards from the right goalpost. This 2-yard section of the goal is the target at which the goalkeeper has to punch the ball. (This means that the balls are not spread all over the pitch afterwards but can be easily collected from the goal.) On the edge of the goal area, in line with the center of the target, is a stack of 5 to 7 tires. The goalkeeper lies 3 yards away from the tires with his feet pointing toward them. The coach is on the edge of the goal area to the right of the right goalpost. He is holding a ball and another 4 balls lie on the ground nearby.

Phase 1

At a call from the coach, the goalkeeper springs to his feet and looks at the coach. At the same time the coach lobs the ball in a high arc so that it falls between the goal line and the tires. The arc must not be too low and the ball must not drop too close to the tires, otherwise the goalkeeper will not be able to punch it with outstretched arms.

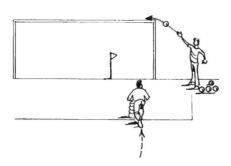

• Tires

113

Phase 2

The goalkeeper dives over the stack of tires, either from a standing position or after taking one pace forward, and punches the ball with both fists. After landing he sprints back and resumes his starting position, and so on.

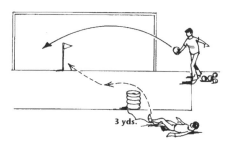

Variations

1. Instead of on his back, the goalkeeper can lie on his front with his legs pointing toward the coach, or perform press-ups, etc.

2. The target is formed by placing a marker flag 2 yards from the left goalpost. The position of the stack of tires remains unchanged. The goalkeeper lies slightly diagonally to the goal line and somewhat further to his right, so that he dives over the tires toward the other side of the goal. The coach must therefore throw the ball further, so that it lands between the left goalpost and the tires.

• Tires

Participants: 1 goalkeeper	**Equipment:**	5 balls
Coach		5 - 7 tires
		1 marker flag
		1 goal area

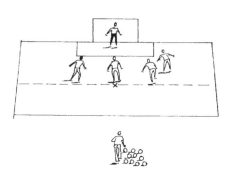

Starting position
The goalkeeper stands in the goal. 4 outfield players stand in the penalty area in a zone bounded by the goal line and an imaginary parallel line that passes through the penalty spot. The coach stands outside the penalty area with 10 balls lying on the ground nearby.

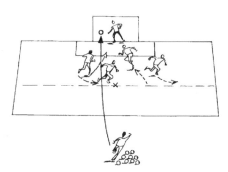

Phase 1
The outfield players constantly change position in the defined zone in the penalty area, hindering the goalkeeper's view. The coach shoots at goal from different angles at different heights and speeds.

Phase 2
The goalkeeper either catches the ball and throws it back to the coach, or punches it away or deflects it to the side. He then sprints back to his starting position, ready for the coach to shoot again.
The coach must ensure that the goalkeeper has to work hard but always has a chance to stop the shots.

• Drills simulating match situations

Variations

1. The outfield players try to deflect the ball.

2. The coach suddenly crosses the ball for one of the outfield players to head at the goal.

3. An outfield player stands about a goal-width away from the coach. The 10 balls are divided equally between the two of them. They either take turns to shoot at the goal or they exchange passes and unleash surprise shots. The goalkeeper is therefore forced to continuously adjust his position as the ball is passed back and forth.

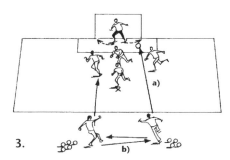

3.

• Drills simulating match situations

Participants:	1 goalkeeper	**Equipment:**	10 balls
	4 outfield players		1 goal
	Coach		penalty area
Variation 3:	5 outfield players		

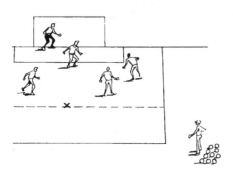

Starting position

The goalkeeper stands in the goal. 4 outfield players stand in the penalty area in a zone bounded by the goal line and an imaginary parallel line that passes through the penalty spot. The coach stands to the right or left of the penalty area. He observes, directs and corrects the players. 10 balls are on the ground nearby.

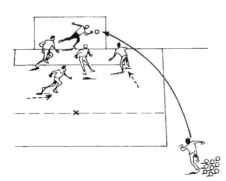

Phase 1

The coach crosses the ball in front of the goal and the outfield players try to impede the goalkeeper as he comes off his line to deal with the ball. They must keep moving, taking up attacking positions, and try to score from the crosses, either by heading or shooting.

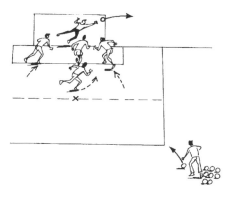

Phase 2

Depending on the situation, the goal-keeper catches or punches the ball, or stays on his line and tries to stop the ensuing shot or header. If he catches the ball he throws it back to the coach. As soon as the goalkeeper resumes his starting position the coach crosses the next ball, and so on.

Variations

1. The coach hits inswinging and outswinging crosses.
2. The coach crosses the ball high or low at random, also varying the speed of the ball.
3. The coach crosses to the near or far post at random.

• Drills simulating match situations

Participants: 1 goalkeeper 4 outfield players Coach	**Equipment:** 10 balls 1 goal penalty area

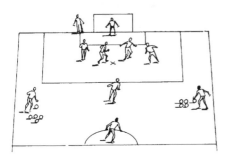

Starting position

The goalkeeper stands in the goal. 4 outfield players stand in the penalty area in a zone bounded by the goal line and an imaginary parallel line that passes through the penalty spot. They are strikers. On each flank is a winger. 5 balls lie near each winger. Another attacker is positioned just outside the penalty area. A target man stands near the center line. The coach stands near the goal. He observes, directs and corrects the players.

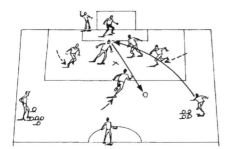

Phase 1

The right winger crosses the ball in front of the goal. The 4 attackers try to lay the ball back to the attacker outside the penalty area. Depending on the situation the goalkeeper stays on his line or tries to get to the ball before the attackers.

Phase 2

The attacker just outside the penalty area runs onto the ball when it is laid back and tries to score with a first-time shot. The 4 attackers are in continuous motion, impeding the goalkeeper's line of sight and trying to deflect the ball and change its path. If the goalkeeper catches the ball he throws it out to the target man, who has made a run toward the left wing.

Drills simulating match situations

119

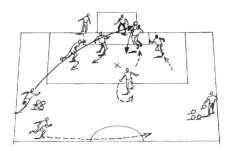

Phase 3

As soon as the goalkeeper resumes his starting position the left winger crosses the ball. The other attackers have also resumed their starting positions. If the goalkeeper catches the ball he throws it out to the target man, who is making a run to the right wing this time.

Variation

To increase the degree of difficulty for the goalkeeper, the attackers can sometimes try to score directly from a cross rather than laying it back.

• Drills simulating match situations

Participants:	1 goalkeeper	Equipment:	10 balls
	8 outfield players		1 goal
	Coach		1 half of the field

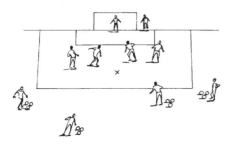

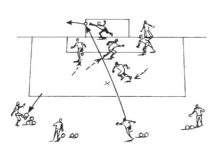

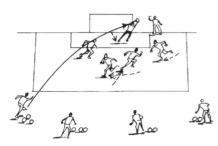

Drills simulating match situations

Starting position

The goalkeeper stands in the goal. 4 outfield players stand in the penalty area in a zone bounded by the goal line and an imaginary parallel line that passes through the penalty spot. They are strikers. On each flank is a winger. Another 2 attackers are positioned outside the penalty area, one in line with the right goalpost and the other in line with the left goalpost. 3 balls are on the ground near each of them and each of the 2 wingers. The coach stands near the goal. He observes, directs and corrects the players.

Phase 1

The right winger crosses the ball in front of the goal. The 4 attackers impede the goalkeeper and try to score from the cross with a header or shot. Depending on the situation the goalkeeper stays on his line or tries to get to the ball before the attackers. If he catches the ball he throws it to the left winger.

Phase 2

As soon as the goalkeeper has resumed his starting position the right attacker outside the penalty area who is in line with the right goalpost shoots at goal. The 4 attackers are in continuous motion, impeding the goalkeeper's line of sight and trying to deflect the ball and change its path. The goalkeeper tries to stop the ball. If the goalkeeper catches the ball he throws it back to the attacker.

Phase 3

As soon as the goalkeeper has dealt with the shot, the outside left crosses the ball, and so on (similar to Phase 1). If the goalkeeper catches the ball he throws it to the right winger.

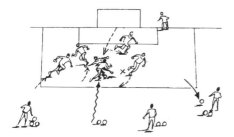

Phase 4

The left attacker outside the penalty area waits until the goalkeeper resumes his starting position, runs with the ball into the penalty area and tries to take the ball past the goalkeeper. The 4 attackers in front of goal leave a channel free for him. The goalkeeper leaves his line quickly and comes to meet the attacker so that he can block his route as far away from the goal as possible. He narrows the angle so that the attacker is forced to try to dribble round him. When the goalkeeper is just short of the attacker he stops his forward movement, sinks into a low squatting position and tries to separate the attacker from the ball by blocking it with his foot or by throwing himself at the attacker's feet or by knocking the ball away with his hand or foot. He subsequently resumes his starting position on the goal line and the right winger then crosses the next ball.

The goalkeeper must always try to defend his goal against every goal-scoring attempt. The speed of the sequence of goal-scoring attempts must be such that the goalkeeper is always under pressure but always has a chance to defend his goal. The goalkeeper must also be coached to work on his weak points.

Variations

1. The following sequence can be used: cross from the right, shot at goal, run at goal, cross from the left, run at goal, shot at goal, cross from the right, etc.

2. To practice with inswinging crosses, the ball can be crossed from the right by a left-footed player and from the left by a right-footed player.

3. After each sequence the 2 attackers in front of goal and outside the penalty area swap roles.

4. The 4 attackers in the penalty area can occasionally lay back a cross to the player outside the penalty area who is not next in the sequence.

5. Except for the attacker who is next in the sequence, all of the attackers must keep a close watch on the goalkeeper's defensive actions and adjust their positions appropriately to be able to take advantage of a rebound. If the goalkeeper punches or deflects a ball and it remains in play, they must try to score with a first-time shot.

• Drills simulating match situations

Participants:	1 goalkeeper	Equipment:	12 balls
	8 outfield players		1 goal
	Coach		1 half of the field

Key aspects

- Agility
- Diving to stop low balls
- Diving to stop high to medium-high balls
- Take-off strength
- Reaction speed
- Catching the ball securely
- Speed off the mark
- Throwing the ball into play

Variations 2
- Rolling away to the side

Variations 6
- Two-fisted punching

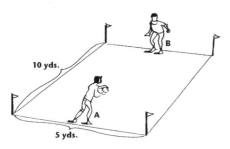

Starting position

Two goals are formed by marker flags. The goals are 5 yards wide and 10 yards apart. A goalkeeper stands in each goal. Goalkeeper A holds a ball.

Phase 1

Goalkeeper A tries to score a goal by rolling the ball at the goal defended by goalkeeper B.

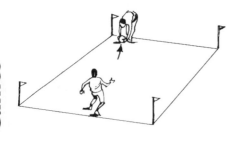

Phase 2

Goalkeeper B takes fast, short steps forward or to the side so that he can pick it up while remaining on his feet. He goes back to the center of his goal and tries to score by rolling the ball at the goal defended by goalkeeper A, and so on.

Rules of the game:
Each goalkeeper rolls the ball 20 times. The winner is the goalkeeper who scores the most goals.

• **Games**

Variations

1. Goalkeeper A throws the ball between knee and head-high at the goal defended by goalkeeper B. Goalkeeper B moves to the ball and catches it while remaining on his feet.

2. Goalkeeper A bounces the ball at the goal defended by goalkeeper B.

3. Goalkeeper B squats in the middle of his goal. Goalkeeper A throws the ball low, high or medium-high toward one side of the goal. Goalkeeper B dives and tries to catch the ball.

4. Goalkeeper B stands beside his right goalpost. Goalkeeper A throws the ball low, high or medium-high toward the left (right) side of the goal. As goalkeeper A throws, goalkeeper B runs across the goal and dives to try to catch the ball.

5. Goalkeeper A drops the ball and half-volleys it at or to the side of goalkeeper B.

6. Goalkeeper A bounces the ball at head height or higher toward goalkeeper B. Goalkeeper B punches the ball with 2 fists, either from a standing position or as he jumps forward. Goalkeeper B tries to score a goal by punching the ball into goalkeeper A's goal. Goalkeeper A tries to catch the ball while remaining on his feet or by diving to it. After 10 throws the goalkeepers swap roles.

• Games

Participants: 2 goalkeepers	**Equipment:** 1 ball
	4 marker flags

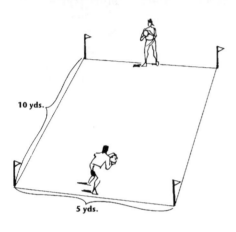

Starting position

Two goals are formed by marker flags. The goals are 5 yards wide and 10 yards apart. A goalkeeper stands in each goal. Each goalkeeper holds a ball.

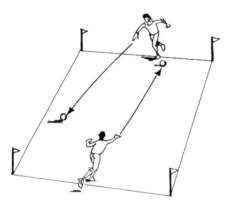

Phase 1

The goalkeepers throw the balls simultaneously, each trying to score in the other's goal.

● Games

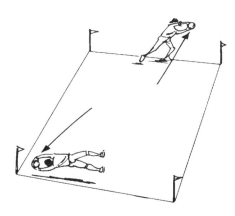

Phase 2

The goalkeepers must try to catch the ball securely in both hands. After catching the ball, each goalkeeper immediately throws again, trying to put the other under pressure. They throw randomly low, high or medium-high or bounce the ball, aiming to the right or left of the other or straight at him.

Rules of the game:

Each goalkeeper scores a point when he scores a goal or when the other goalkeeper cannot catch the ball in both hands.

• Games

Participants: 2 goalkeepers	Equipment:	2 balls
		4 marker flags

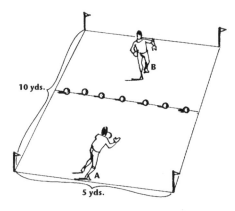

Starting position

4 marker flags are placed to form a playing area 5 yards wide and 10 yards long. The center line is marked by 7 balls. Goalkeeper A stands on the line at one end of the playing area. He is holding a ball. Goalkeeper B is in the other half of the playing area.

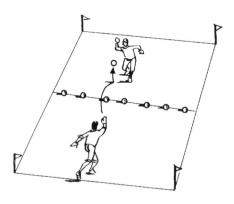

Phase 1

Goalkeepers A holds the ball with one hand in front of his body. With the other hand, which is open and curved (fingers and thumbs together) he hits the ball into the half of goalkeeper B.

• **Games**

Phase 2

Goalkeeper B moves toward the ball, allows it to bounce once in his half, then uses one hand to hit it back into the other half. Goalkeeper A tries to hit it back, and so on. The goalkeepers must try to hit the ball so that it cannot be hit back. They can run forward and back, dive forward and to the side and roll to the side in their efforts to reach the ball and hit it back.

Rules of the game:

Points are scored as in table tennis. Each goalkeeper serves 5 times in succession from the line at the back of his half. The ball can only be played with one hand. If the ball touches one of the balls on the center line, this is a fault.

Variation

The center line is marked by a length of cord, which is strung at a height of 30 to 70 cm between 2 marker flags.

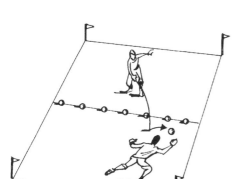

Participants: 2 goalkeepers	Equipment:	8 balls
		4 marker flags
	Variations:	1 ball
		6 marker flags
		1 length of cord

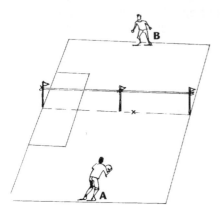

Starting position

A cord is strung at a height of 1 to 10 yards between 3 marker flags, separating the penalty area into 2 halves. The 2 goalkeepers stand at the center of the 2 lines that usually form the left and right sides of the penalty area. Goalkeeper A holds a ball.

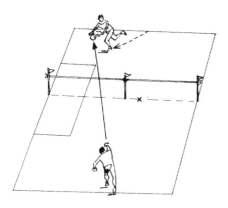

Phase 1

Goalkeeper A throws the ball over the cord into goalkeeper B's half. Goalkeeper B sprints to the ball and tries to catch it, either remaining on his feet or diving, before it touches the ground.

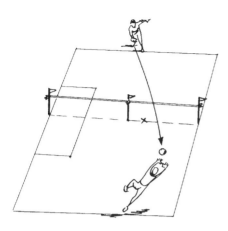

Phase 2

Goalkeeper B goes back to his starting position and throws the ball into the half of goalkeeper A, and so on.

Rules of the game:

A point is scored when the ball is thrown outside the playing area or under the cord, or touches the ground in one of the halves of the playing area, or rebounds from the goalkeeper's hands.

Participants: 2 goalkeepers	Equipment:	1 ball
		penalty area
		3 marker flags
		1 cord

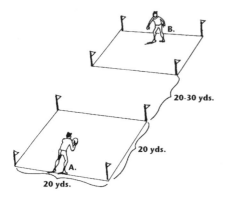

Starting position

Each goalkeeper has a zone measuring 20 x 20 yards with a marker flag at each corner. Between the 2 zones is a free zone, which separates the zones by 20 to 30 yards. The goalkeepers stand in their zones. Goalkeeper A stands on the line marking the back of his zone. He is holding a ball.

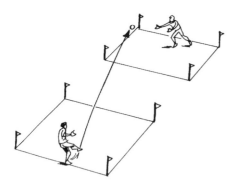

Phase 1

Goalkeeper A drops the ball and half-volleys it over the free zone and into goalkeeper B's zone.

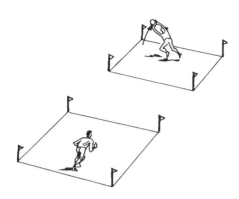

Phase 2

Goalkeeper B tries to catch the ball before it touches the ground in his zone. He can either remain on his feet or dive to catch the ball. He then half-volleys the ball back into goalkeeper A's zone from the spot where he caught it, and so on.

Rules of the game:
A point is scored when the ball is played outside the goalkeepers' zones, touches the ground inside a goalkeeper's zone, or is not caught properly. After a point is scored, play is resumed from the line at the back of the zone.

Variation

The ball is volleyed or thrown instead of half-volleyed. The size of the free zone is increased or decreased accordingly

• Games

| **Participants:** 2 goalkeepers | **Equipment:** 1 ball |
| | 8 marker flags |

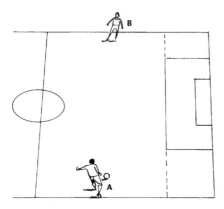

Starting position

The goalkeepers play the game across the pitch in the area between the penalty area and the center line. Goalkeeper A stands at one side of the pitch with the ball 2 yards in front of him. Goalkeeper B is on the line at the other side of the pitch.

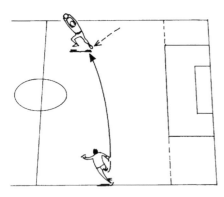

Phase 1

Goalkeeper A runs up and kicks the ball to the other side of the pitch. Goalkeeper B runs to meet the ball and tries to catch it before it touches the ground.

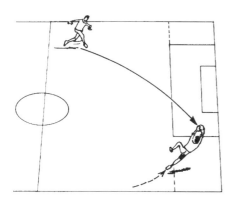

Phase 2

If goalkeeper B catches the ball, he is allowed to drop-kick it to the other side of the pitch. If the ball touches the ground before he catches it, he has to place the ball on the ground at the point where he caught it and then kick it across the pitch. If the ball crosses the sideline, goalkeeper B is allowed to volley the ball from this spot toward the opposite sideline. Goalkeeper A runs to meet the ball and tries to catch it before it touches the ground, and so on.

Rules of the game:
When the ball crosses the opposite sideline, this counts as a goal. After a goal is scored the ball is kicked from the ground.

Variation

If the ball touches the ground, it must be thrown from the spot where it touched.

● Games

| Participants: 2 goalkeepers | Equipment: | 1 ball |
| | | 1 half of the field |

Starting position

The goalkeeper stands in his goal. The coach is standing just outside the penalty area. Near the coach lie 10 balls.

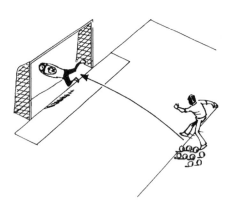

Phase 1

The coach shoots at the goal. The goalkeeper tries to stop the shot, catching the ball securely if possible. If he cannot catch it he can punch it away or deflect it to the side or over the crossbar. If he catches the ball he rolls it back to the coach.

• Games

135

Phase 2

The goalkeeper resumes his starting position and the coach immediately shoots again. The coach shoots in rapid sequence to keep the goalkeeper under pressure, but always gives the goalkeeper a chance of stopping the ball. The coach shoots from different positions, varying the speed, height and direction of the shots.

Rules of the game:
The coach wins a point for every goal that he scores. The goalkeeper scores a point for every save and every shot that is wide of the goal.

Variations

1. The coach kicks the ball at goal from the ground and from his hands alternately.
2. Goalkeeper A recuperates actively by moving back and forth around the penalty spot, impeding the view of goalkeeper B and diverting the ball from its path when possible.

• Games

Participants:	1 goalkeeper	Equipment:	10 balls
	Coach		1 goal
Variation 2:	2 goalkeepers		penalty area

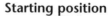

Starting position

The goalkeeper stands in the middle of his goal. 10 balls lie at intervals of 18 inches along the front edge of the goal area. The coach stands about 13 yards in front of the goal.

Phase 1

The goalkeeper sprints to the ball at the left end of the line and kicks it with the inside of his foot to the coach.

Phase 2

As the goalkeeper sprints back to his goal, the coach hits a powerful first-time shot at the goal. The goalkeeper tries to stop the shot. He can catch it, deflect it to the side or punch it away. If he catches the ball he plays it away to the side. After dealing with the shot he sprints immediately to the next ball and plays it to the coach, and so on. The goalkeeper must always sprint as fast he can between the balls and his goal so that the coach can keep him under pressure. The coach varies the direction and height of the shots.

Rules of the game:
The coach wins a point for every goal he scores. The goalkeeper scores a point for every save and every shot that is wide of the goal.

Games

137

Variations

1. The balls lie next to each other in a line 10 yards away from the goal. The coach stands on the edge of the penalty area. Because the goalkeeper has to run further, the coach can control the pass from the goalkeeper and delay his shot, so that he can lob the ball over the goalkeeper as he retreats toward the goal.

2. After starting off from his goal line, the goalkeeper performs a forward roll on his path to the ball.

3. Immediately after passing the ball to the coach, the goalkeeper performs a backward roll. He must try to stop the coach's shot as he comes out of the backward roll.

4. The balls lie in a semi-circle in front of goal. The semi-circle stretches from the points where the sides of the penalty meet the goal line to the penalty spot. The goalkeeper runs to a ball, picks it up, throws it medium-high to the coach and sprints back to the goal. The coach, who stands outside of the penalty area, catches the ball and lobs it over the goalkeeper's head toward the goal.

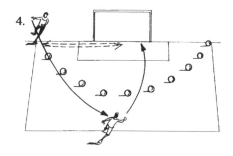

● **Games**

Participants: 1 goalkeeper	Equipment:	10 balls
Coach		1 goal
		penalty area

Starting position

The goalkeeper stands in the middle of his goal. He is holding a ball. Another 5 balls lie in his goal. An outfield player stands outside the goal area in line with the left (or right) goalpost.

Phase 1

The goalkeeper throws the ball in a high arc to the outfield player, so that the outfield player can stand or jump and head it at the goal.

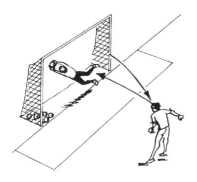

Phase 2

The outfield player tries to head the ball just inside the left goalpost. He can head it high or medium-high or even downward so that it bounces in front of the goal. The goalkeeper dives to stop it immediately or after taking a short step. He can catch the ball, punch it away or deflect it. He picks up another ball and resumes his starting position, and so on.

Rules of the game:
The goalkeeper scores a point for every save and every shot that is wide of the goal. The outfield player gets a point for every goal he scores.

• Games

Participants:	1 goalkeeper		**Equipment:**	6 balls
	1 outfield player			1 goal
				1 goal area

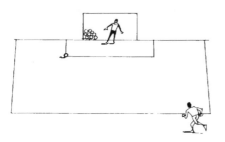

Starting position

The goalkeeper stands in the middle of his goal. A ball is positioned on the left (or right) corner of the goal area. Another 9 balls lie in the goal beside the left (or right) goalpost. An outfield player stands just outside the right (or left) corner of the penalty area.

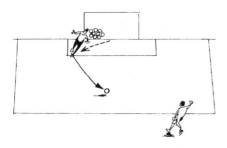

Phase 1

The goalkeeper takes a goal kick, sending the ball low, high or medium-high to the outfield player.

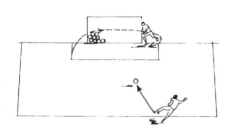

Phase 2

After kicking the ball, the goalkeeper turns toward the left (or right) goalpost and sprints round the back of the goal. At the same time the outfield player controls the ball that the goalkeeper kicked to him and shoots at the deserted goal. The outfield player must not enter the penalty area.

• Games

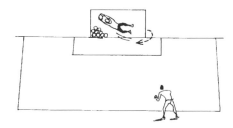

Phase 3

The goalkeeper tries to stop the shot. He can catch the ball, punch it away or deflect it. He places the ball, or one of the balls lying in the goal, ready for a goal kick, and so on.

Rules of the game:
The outfield player gets a point for every goal he scores. The goalkeeper scores a point for every save and every shot that is wide of the goal.

Variations

1. The goalkeeper takes the goal kicks from the other side of the goal and the outfield player stands on the other side of the penalty area.
2. The goalkeeper stands in the middle of his goal. He throws the ball to the outfield player.

• **Games**

Participants:	1 goalkeeper	Equipment:	10 balls
	1 outfield player		1 goal
			penalty area

The authors

Gerd Thissen
Born 1951. Teacher of sport and French. Soccer teacher.

Scientific research and teaching assistant at the Institute for Sports Science of Aachen University of Technology since 1976. At the sociology department of Heinrich Heine University, Düsseldorf, since 1990. Member of the faculty of sports science of the Ruhr University, Bochum, since 1996.

Has coached youth, amateur and university soccer teams since 1968. Won the German University Championship 3 times with the Aachen University of Technology team. Teaches and lectures to coaches at regional and national soccer training courses and the annual courses of the Association of German Soccer Teachers.

Author of several books on the theory and practice of soccer with special emphasis on children's and youth soccer, goalkeeper coaching, teaching tactics and soccer-specific physical exercise.

Since 1997, West German Soccer Association's representative for cooperation between schools and clubs and member of the "General Coaching Plan for Child and Youth Soccer Players" Commission and the School Soccer Committee of the West German Soccer Association.

Publisher of sports books on soccer and ice hockey.

Klaus Röllgen
Born 1932. Graduate sports teacher.

Sports teacher with the Mittelrhein Soccer Association until 1998.

National winner of the German Soccer Association cup with the Mittelrhein Soccer Association team in 1974.

Author of several books on the coaching of technique and tactics in competitive soccer.

Employed by the German Soccer Association as a teacher of coaches. Lecturer at the national training courses of the Association of German Soccer Teachers and at coaches' congresses outside Germany.

President of the Association of German Soccer Teachers since 1994.